A
GOURMET'S
GUIDE TO

SHELLFISH

SHELLFISH

MARY CADOGAN

Photography by
DAVID GILL

HPBooks
a division of
PRICE STERN SLOAN
Los Angeles

Another Best-Selling Volume from HPBooks

© Salamander Books Ltd., 1990

Published by HPBooks
A division of Price Stern Sloan, Inc.
360 North La Cienega Boulevard
Los Angeles, CA 90048

9 8 7 6 5 4 3 2 1

Notice: Certain shellfish are highly poisonous and can cause serious illness or death. This cookbook is *not* to be used as a scientific guide to shellfish. To the best of our knowledge the information contained in this book is accurate, however neither the author nor HPBooks, a division of Price Stern Sloan, Inc., make any warranties or representations concerning such information. The author and publisher expressly disclaim any liability in connection with the use of this information. As with many foods, certain shellfish invoke allergies or adverse reactions in some people. For more information regarding these dangers, consult your physician or local poison control center.

By arrangement with Salamander Books Ltd., and Merehurst Press, London

Library of Congress Cataloging-in-Publication Data

Cadogan, Mary (Mary Lucia)
    A gourmet's guide to shellfish / Mary Cadogan ; photographed by David Gill.
        p.   c.m.
     ISBN 0-89586-850-4
     1. Cookery (Shellfish)   I. Title.
TX753.C33   1990
641.6'94—dc20   89-78363
                                  CIP

This book was commissioned and directed by Merehurst Limited.
Ferry House, 51/57 Lacy Road, London SW15 1PR
Photography: David Gill
Home Economists: Mary Cadogan and Maxine Clark
Stylist: Maria Kelly
Color separation by Scantrans Pte. Ltd., Singapore
Printed in Belgium by Proost International Book Production, Turnhout

Recognizing the importance of preserving that which has been written, Price Stern Sloan, Inc. has decided to print this book on acid-free paper, and will continue to print the majority of the books it publishes on acid-free paper.

Contents

Introduction

The world of shellfish must surely be one of the most exciting for the gourmet cook. Crustaceans, mollusks and edible sea creatures of all kinds show off their wondrous shapes and colors and, as fishing and transport become more sophisticated, so the variety available increases. As the seasons change it seems there is always something new to inspire us. Shellfish are however surrounded in mystery. Which part of a crab is edible, how do I check if a mussel is really fresh, what is the best way to tackle an octopus? These and many other questions are answered in this book.

Here you will find all the main shellfish varieties clearly photographed with a wealth of information about each. Step-by-step photography guides you through preparation and cooking techniques to give you confidence to deal with the shellfish you may wish to cook.

The dictionary describes a gourmet as a 'judge of good eating.' Where shellfish are concerned I feel that the simple approach is usually the best. A few well chosen ingredients, lovingly cooked and carefully presented, are all that you need to enhance the subtle tastes and delicate textures of shellfish. What could be simpler than a delicious grilled lobster strewn with herbs and green peppercorns, or a steaming plate of mussels with aromatic juices just waiting to be mopped up? These are truly gourmet feasts. I hope that you will feel inspired to try them and the many other recipes in this book.

Razor shell clam

Mollusks

Mollusks are invertebrates, protected by a strong outer shell. They can be classified into *Gastropoda*—creatures living in single shells—and *Lamellibranchiata* or bivalves—those with double-hinged shells.

Gastropoda include limpets, cockles, whelks and periwinkles. They are a small, modest group of creatures, not renowned for their great eating qualities. The mirex, also called *escargot de mer*, is a member of this group too; although its eating qualities are poor, it is the source of a purple dye thought to have been discovered by Heracles. The empty mirex shell is a popular home for the hermit crab.

Bivalves are a much larger group and include oysters, clams, mussels, scallops, abalone and razor shells. Many of the mollusks in this group are caught in great abundance, but tend to be ignored. The oyster alone does not suffer neglect—its subtle flavor is renowned the world over.

Mollusks tend to be estuary- or shore-dwelling creatures. Bivalves, such as mussels and oysters, are often found clinging to rocks at the mouth of rivers. As they cannot move voluntarily they usually stay on the same rock for the whole of their lives. Cockles, periwinkles and whelks can leap short distances and they move by the thousands with the tide. Clams and cockles are usually harvested from beaches at low tide.

Mollusks are usually eaten raw or very briefly cooked. They must therefore be very fresh. Mussels, oysters and clams are usually sold live. Their shells must be tightly closed and any that are open should be tapped sharply. If the shell closes they are fine to eat; if it remains open this means that the shellfish is dead and must be discarded.

Because mollusks such as mussels and clams tend to live in shallow sandy waters, they tend to take sand and other particles into their shell when they feed. When placed in a bucket of cold salted water with a sprinkling of oatmeal or flour, the shellfish will feed on the oatmeal and excrete the dirt. Scrub the mollusk shell thoroughly using a stiff brush to remove grit and barnacles.

Oysters are usually eaten raw, in the half shell with their juices. Cockles and razor shells can also be eaten raw and are often sprinkled with lemon juice or vinegar. Most other mollusks are cooked before eating. Mussels and clams are usually steamed in their own juices, but they are also delicious baked and stuffed, or used in soups and stews. The delicate flavored scallop requires careful cooking to protect its soft texture. It is often poached or steamed and served with a creamy sauce.

Cockles, periwinkles and whelks are generally sold cooked and are eaten more in Britain than in America. Serve them cold with vinegar and brown bread and butter in the traditional style of the true Londoner.

Selection of mollusks: oysters, cockles, whelks, scallops, clams, mussels and periwinkles

Clam

Clams are available throughout the year but are at their best in the autumn. There are more clam species available in North America than Europe and they are extremely popular in America, particularly the soft-shell and hard-shell clams. Many of the American clams have European relatives, but they are less popular.

The soft-shell clam *(Mya arenaria)*, also called longneck or steamer, is harvested from the North Atlantic to North Carolina and from Britain to France. The shell is dirty fawn or white.

Soft-shell clams have thin, brittle shells with a gap at each end. Because of this, they are often sandy and gritty and need particularly thorough cleaning (see below).

The hard-shell clam *(Mercenaria mercenaria)*, also known as quahog or littleneck, originally came from North America, but has been colonized in many places around the Mediterranean and Ireland. It has an oval shell which is dull grey or brown outside and purple inside.

The surf or bar clam *(Spisula solidissima)*, native to North America, is a large clam up to 6 inches across with a smooth, creamy, brown shell. Because of its size it is usually chopped or minced for use in chowder, or sliced and deep-fried.

The wedge shell *(Donax trunculus)* is plentiful in the Mediterranean. The small clam is closely related to some American species, including the bean clam *(Donax spp.)*. The shell may be white, yellow, purple or brown.

The carpet shell *(Venerupis decussata)*, is a small clam up to 3 inches across. It is white, yellow or light brown and a native of Britain and the Mediterranean. It is excellent and much sought after. It can be eaten raw like an oyster. The smaller golden carpet shell *(Venerupis aurea)* is also popular.

The venus shell *(Callista chione)* has a smooth shiny reddish brown decorative shell. It is caught from southern Britain to the Mediterranean and is similar to the carpet shell, although a little larger. It can be cooked or eaten raw.

The smaller, warty venus *(Venus verrucosa)* is caught in the same waters and is greatly appreciated in Mediterranean countries. This clam is called *vongola* in Italy and is the one used in the famous *vongole* sauce for pasta.

Buying & Storing
Because clams are cooked only briefly or eaten raw, they must be absolutely fresh when you buy them. They are sold live in the shell and should be eaten within 24 hours. Put them in a bucket of clean water with a sprinkling of oatmeal or cornmeal, leave for 24 hours, then scrub shells under cold running water with a stiff brush. Discard any with broken or gaping shells.

Preparation
To open a clam, use a strong sharp knife to pry the shell open and sever the hinge. Discard the top shell if serving raw. If you want to remove the clam completely from the shell, insert the point of the knife between the clam and the shell and cut the clam free. Pick out any pieces of broken shell and rinse the clam thoroughly.

To cook clams in the shell, put into a large saucepan with enough water just to cover the bottom of the pan. Cover tightly and cook 3 to 8 minutes, depending on size and number of clams, shaking the pan occasionally, until the shells have opened. Discard any that haven't.

Serving Suggestions
Clams are usually steamed like mussels in their own juices, and the liquor served as a broth to dip bread or the clams into. They are often eaten raw like oysters, too.

They are particularly good in soups and chowders; baked and stuffed in their half shells; used in sauces to serve with rice or pasta; battered and deep-fried; or in pies.

Clams can also be used in any recipe calling for mussels or oysters, although they do not have as delicate a flavor as oysters.

Hard-shell clam (large)

Littleneck clam

Quahog clam

Soft-shell clam

Warty Venus clam

Carpet shell clam

Golden carpet shell clam

Mussel

The mussel is a familiar sight in fish stalls and markets throughout the autumn and winter. Often called the poor man's oyster it provides a delicious meal at relatively low cost. The name mussel is derived from the Latin word *mus* meaning mousse, perhaps because of its shape.

The thin crescent-shaped shell of the common mussel *(Mytilus edulis)* is usually dark blue or blackish, but some varieties can be paler with dark brown or purple marking. The mussels cling in clusters to rocks, although commercially they are more likely to be hanging from ropes attached to stakes in mussel farms.

Musselburgh, in Scotland, once the site of a Roman camp, owes its name to the mussel beds located at the mouth of the river Esk.

Mussels sold commercially are collected from waters that are known to be clean, although they should still be carefully rinsed before eating. An area around the north Norfolk coastline from Brancaster to Blakeney is the only EEC pollution-free harbor in Britain where mussel farming is allowed. From May onwards the mussel spawn is collected from the sandbanks and taken to holding pits where they are left to fatten in the clear water. It is inadvisable to collect mussels in the wild as they may be affected by pollution.

Mussels are generally sold live in the shell, but they are also available frozen, in or out of the shell; canned or in jars in brine; or sometimes fresh, cooked and shelled.

Cultivated mussels vary in size, color and flavor and there is great disagreement about where the best flavored mussel comes from. They are cultivated extensively in France, Spain, the Netherlands and along the American Atlantic coastline.

The New Zealand greenlip mussel *(Perna canaliculata)* is large and has a particularly rich flavor. It is available fresh, frozen or canned in Australia, New Zealand and the United States.

The horse mussel *(Modiolus modiolus)* is another large mussel, harvested in the North Atlantic. The shell is purplish-yellow and the flesh is orange. It does not have such a good flavor as the common mussel and is best used in robustly flavored sauces.

The fan mussel *(Pinna fragilis,* var. *Pinna pectinata),* also called pen shell or sea wing, is the largest of the British bivalves and can measure over 14 inches across. The yellow-brown shell has a pointed end which it buries in the sand. It can be cooked like a scallop.

Buying & Storing

When buying live mussels, check that the shells are tightly closed. Open shells indicate that the mussel inside is dead and should not be eaten. Store for up to 24 hours in a bucket of cold water in a cool place. Discard any that have opened or that float at the end of this time.

If time allows, sprinkle a little oatmeal or flour on the water: the mussels will feed on the oatmeal and excrete their dirt.

Preparation

Scrub shells thoroughly and remove any barnacles or weeds with a strong knife. Pull off the fibrous beard attached to each shell. Rinse again in clear water. Discard any that are open and do not close when tapped sharply, and any with damaged shells.

To cook, put mussels in a large saucepan with a little water or wine. Cover and cook 3 to 5 minutes, depending on size and number of mussels, until shells have opened; discard any that do not open.

Serving Suggestions

Mussels are most often steamed in their own juices or with wine and garlic *à la marinière.*

After the preparatory cooking described above they can also be wrapped in bacon and grilled; baked in the open shell with parsley, bread crumbs and garlic, pesto or tomato sauce; added to soups; mixed with tomato sauce and served with pasta; and used with other fish and shellfish in seafood casseroles.

Mussels can also be used as a substitute for clams.

New Zealand greenlip mussel (cooked)

Common mussel, Spanish (uncooked)

Common mussel (cooked)

Common mussel (uncooked)

Oyster

Until the 19th century oysters were an everyday food eaten by the poor to eke out expensive meat. But because of over-fishing they are now comparatively rare and have become a luxury seafood with a high price. The culture of oysters can be traced back to classical times; shells have been found in the ancient ruins of Roman times when they were fattened in tanks and cultured to ensure a good supply.

The European oyster (*Ostrea edulis*) is considered to have the best flavor, with the English native oyster being the most prized. It has a greyish-brown, irregular shell, reaching up to 4 inches.

European oysters are found from the Norwegian sea down to the Mediterranean and Morocco. They are cultured in many places along the coasts of England, France, Belgium and the Netherlands. They are also grown in beds along the U.S. coast. These oysters are best served raw in the half shell with just a squeeze of lemon juice.

The less worthy Portuguese oyster (*Crassostrea angulata*) is elongated, reaching up to 6-1/2 inches. Although it can be eaten raw, it is not as good as the European oyster and is therefore best used in cooked dishes.

On the east coast of the United States, you will find the American or Eastern oyster (*Crassostrea virginica*). This species has a rough, greyish shell and reaches 6-1/2 inches in length. It is relatively abundant and is used in a wide variety of ways, including soups, stews and casseroles.

The giant Pacific oyster (*Crassostrea gigas*) is a large oyster from the Orient which can reach 10 inches in length. It has been successfully introduced to several areas of the Pacific coast of North America. It is also called the Japanese oyster.

Olympia oysters are native to the Pacific coast of North America and are prized for their delicate flavor and small size. Unfortunately their popularity has made them very scarce.

Buying & Storing

Oysters are not normally available during the summer months, when spawning makes then appear fatter, as they contain eggs, and they are less succulent to eat.

Oysters are sold by the dozen in the shell or half shell. If bought in the shell, they should be live with the shells tightly closed; discard any that do not close when tapped—this means they are dead. If bought in the half shell, they should be plump, a natural creamy color with clear shiny liquid and a pleasant sea smell. They should be eaten on the day that they are purchased.

Oysters can be bought fresh in jars and cans, or smoked in cans.

Preparation

If bought in the shell, scrub under cold running water to remove the sand.

To open an oyster, hold firmly in paper towels or a napkin on a work surface, with the flatter shell uppermost and hinged end towards you. Insert the point of an oyster knife into the gap in the hinge linking the shells. Twist knife blade firmly to snap the shells apart.

Work knife along inside of upper shell to sever muscle holding the shells together. Discard top shell, retaining as much liquid in lower shell as possible.

To free the oyster, work knife under oyster to cut through muscle holding it to lower shell.

Serving Suggestions

Allow 6 to 12 oysters per person and serve on a bed of cracked ice, with lemon. Oysters are also very good wrapped in bacon and broiled; sprinkled with bread crumbs and parsley and lightly broiled; or stuffed with spinach and cooked, as Oysters Rockefeller (see page 65).

Smoked oysters are good as part of a starter, a garnish and in salads.

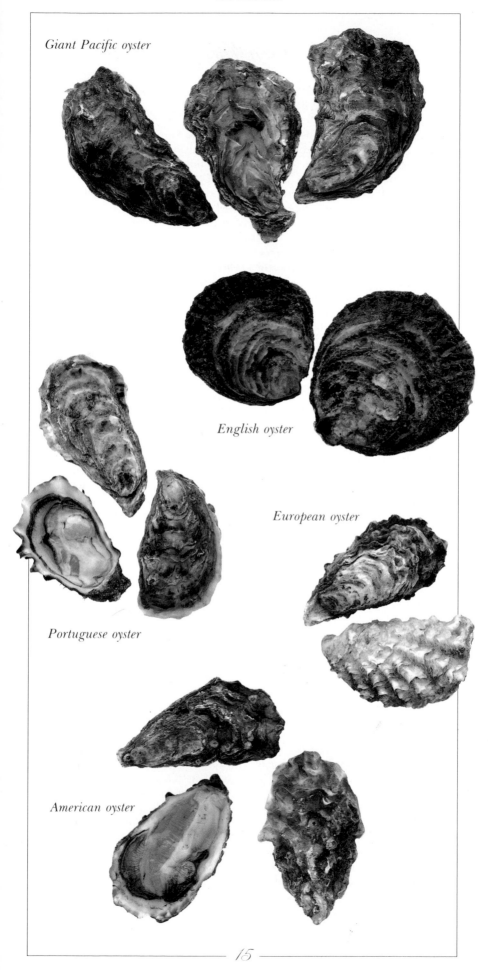

Giant Pacific oyster

English oyster

European oyster

Portuguese oyster

American oyster

Scallop

Scallops are among the most sought after seafood. They have a delectable flavor and soft texture. Available throughout the winter, they are at their best during the coldest months.

Scallops swim around by opening and closing their shells to propel themselves through the water. The white muscle joining the upper and lower shells is therefore relatively large and powerful.

Most scallops are hermaphrodites, each containing an orange roe (or coral) and whitish testis. Their fan-shaped, ridged shell makes an attractive container for seafood starters; Coquille St. Jacques is baked in the shells.

The edible part is the large white muscle and the coral attached to it, although in America the coral is not normally eaten. All other parts, including the frilly mantle surrounding the muscle, are discarded. The initial preparation is usually done by the fishmongers.

The sea scallop (*Pecten maximus*), or king scallop, is the most common variety. It has a pinkish- or whitish-brown shell that is up to 6 inches in diameter.

The queen scallop (*Pecten opercularis*), is a small scallop with an almost circular shell. It is found in deeper waters than the sea scallop and fishing for it is a comparatively new development. The roe is usually a vivid orange red.

Both of these can be eaten throughout the year but are at their fattest and best from January to June. There are about 8 sea scallops and approximately 40 queen scallops or 'queenies' as they are often called to 1 pound.

Another small relative of the sea scallop is the pétoncle (*Chlamys varia*). It has a firmer muscle, which is not as white.

The bay scallop (*Argopecten irradians*) is another small scallop which is fished commercially off the American Atlantic coast. It is a great delicacy and can be eaten raw when very fresh. The larger saucer scallop (*Amu-sium balloti*) is a popular Australian species.

Buying & Storing

When buying in the complete shell, select only those scallops that are tightly closed. Scrub the shells under cold running water and let stand in a bucket of cold salted water for an hour to cleanse themselves. Eat within 24 hours.

More usually, scallops are sold cleaned and ready to cook. Look for white meat with no discoloration and a plump coral, if present. Consume on the day of purchase.

Scallops are also available shelled and frozen, often without the coral. They should be thawed slowly, to retain their flavor and texture, then cooked as soon as possible.

Preparation

To open the shell, hold the scallop in a cloth with the flat shell uppermost. Insert a small sharp knife into the small opening between the shells and carefully work it across the inside of the flat shell to sever the muscle. Pry the shells apart. To free the scallop, carefully slide the knife blade under the greyish outer rim of the scallop (this is the mantle). Remove the flesh from the shell and separate the white muscle and orange coral; remove any dark strands with the point of a sharp knife and discard the mantle and other organs. Rinse the muscle and coral and scrub the inside of the deep shell if it is to be used as a cooking vessel.

Serving Suggestions

Scallops need careful cooking to preserve their delicate taste and texture; overcooking renders them tough and rubbery. They are best poached or steamed, but can also be fried or baked under a cheese sauce—as for Coquille St. Jacques.

Scallops are also delicious sautéed briefly in garlic butter and sprinkled with herbs; or wrapped in bacon, sprinkled with lime juice and broiled to perfection.

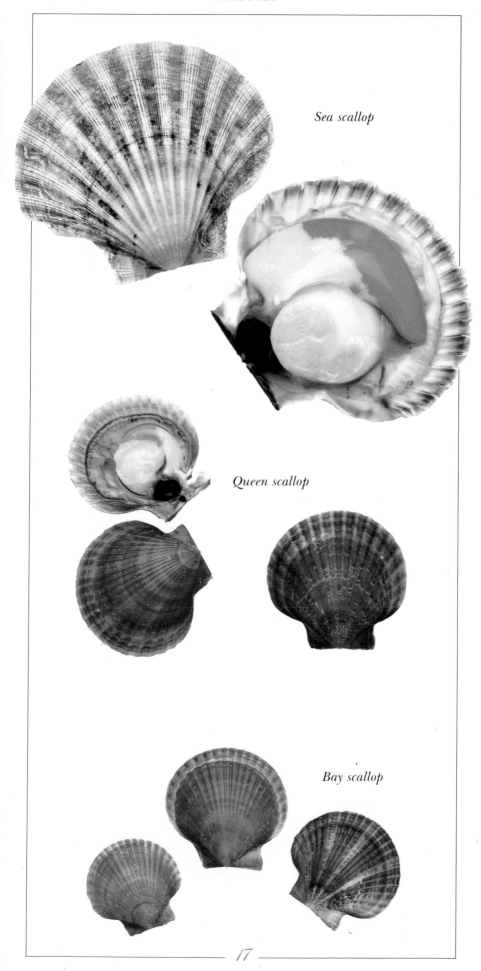

Sea scallop

Queen scallop

Bay scallop

Abalone

The abalone (*Haliotis tuberculata*) or ormer has other common names, including mutton fish, earshell, sea ears and paua (in New Zealand). Abalone used to play an important part in the diet of Aborigines in Australia and Maoris in New Zealand.

The species is called ormer in Britain and the Mediterranean and abalone in North America. The best abalone are thought to be those caught on the Pacific Coast of North America. In Britain the ormer is found only in the Channel Islands.

The abalone is bigger than an oyster, with a maximum length of 5 inches. It is as renowed for its beautiful pearly shell, which is used to make jewelry and ornaments, as for the meat itself. It is said you can tell the age of an abalone by the number of small holes found along the curved edge of the shell.

When the shell is opened it reveals a round white muscle, known as the foot, surrounded by a darker colored frilly muscle called the mantle. The foot is the part which is commonly eaten. The meat needs to be tenderized by beating before being braised or fried.

The main species are the blacklip abalone (*Haliotis ruber*) and the greenlip abalone (*Haliotis laevigata*). The blacklip abalone has a red corrugated shell and is given its name because of the black mantle that surrounds the foot. It lives in crevices, caves and coastal reefs. The greenlip abalone has a red shell streaked with light green and is roughly corrugated. It lives on open rock faces and is said to be the most tender.

Buying & Storing

Abalone can be bought live in the shell, shelled fresh or frozen. Buy live ones if possible as the fresher they are the more tender they will be. To check if one is alive, touch the meat and it will move.

Live abalone can be kept fresh for up to 2 days in a bucket of salted water covered with a damp cloth. If buying shelled abalone, store wrapped in the refrigerator for up to 24 hours.

Preparation

To shell abalone, force the tip of an oyster knife (or other small strong knife) into the thin end of the shell underneath the flesh. Work the blade until the muscle becomes free. Remove the white foot and wash thoroughly. Discard the intestine. The foot may be left whole or cut in thin slices. To tenderize, pound the meat with a mallet until limp and velvety.

Serving Suggestions

Whole tenderized abalone is best braised. Slices of abalone can be quickly stir-fried, or coated in egg and bread crumbs and deep-fried. Finely chopped or minced abalone can be made into fritters or added to soups and chowder. The Chinese sometimes steam abalone in the shell for as long as 10 hours to tenderize.

To cook abalone in the shell, return tenderized meat to cleaned shell, top with grated gingerroot, chile strips and oyster sauce; steam for about 2 hours.

Ocean Quahog

The ocean quahog (*Arctica islandica*) is similar in appearance to the quahog clam (see page 10) but it is not the same species. It is almost circular in shape with a brown-black shell and lives in fairly deep water in sandy mud. It is found from Newfoundland to North Carolina and in European waters, although it is not generally fished in the latter.

The flavor varies greatly according to habitat; some can have a strong unpleasant taste. The flesh is dark, making it unsuitable for use in clam chowders and creamy sauces. Ocean quahog is mainly used in America, in minced clam products and stews.

Abalone

Ocean quahog

Cockle

The cockle (*Cerastaderma edule*) is made up of two ridged, oval shells hinged by a ligament at the pointed end. The shell can be brown, pale yellow or off-white and it reaches a maximum size of 2-1/2 inches across. Cockles are at their best in winter and are usually sold cooked, with or without their shells.

Cockles are often found on the beach, especially at low tide. They are a common sight around the beaches of Britain, particularly in Norfolk and the West Country.

Cerastaderma edule is an inhabitant of British waters; *Cerastaderma glaucum*, in the Mediterranean, is almost identical. Relatives of these include the larger, spiny cockle (*Acanthocardia aculeata*), the prickly cockle (*Acanthocardia echinata*) and *Acanthocardia tuberculata*, called *cuore rossa* in Italy because the animal in the shell is bright red when alive. The dog cockle (*Glycymeris glycymeris*), with its distinctive patterned shell, is found throughout the Mediterranean.

In all there are over 200 varieties of cockles found throughout the world, not all of them worth eating.

The heart shell or heart cockle (*Glossus humanus*) is not a true cockle but looks very similar; it is heart-shaped when viewed sideways. It is found from Iceland and Norway down to the Mediterranean.

Buying & Storing

If you harvest the cockles yourself or buy them live, clean carefully before cooking. Leave them in a bucket of lightly salted water for 1 hour to rid them of sand. Discard any that are not tightly closed. Scrub the shells under cold running water. Live cockles can be kept in a bucket of salted water for up to 24 hours.

Cockles are most often sold ready cooked, either in or out of their shells. The streets of London used to throng with stalls selling cockles dressed with vinegar, but they are now a rare sight, except in some seaside towns.

Preparation

In Britain it is usual to steam cockles briefly in a little water until the shells open, then remove shells and dress the cockles with vinegar.

They can also be poached, broiled, baked or barbecued. Whatever the method, it should take no more than 5 minutes for the shell to open, meaning the cockles are cooked.

Stir-fried cockles are good: shell them as you would an oyster (see page 14), then stir-fry quickly in oil flavored with garlic and herbs.

Serving Suggestions

Cockles make good sauces for pasta and rice, or they can be used in starters or soups.

Razor Shell Clam

Razor shell clams (*Ensis ensis*) are very distinctive: they have long brittle shells resembling the old-fashioned straight razor—hence their name. They gape permanently at both ends, making them impossible to market because of the health hazard. The shells can grow to a length of 5 inches—the creature can protrude from each end. They are found in shallow sandy water. (Illustrated on page 8).

Preparation

Cover with salted water and leave to stand for 1 hour to allow them to rid themselves of sand. Remove clams, change the water and repeat.

To cook, put in a large pan with 1/2 inch of water or wine. Bring to a boil, cover and shake pan for about 2 minutes, until shells open; discard any that do not. The meat can then be stir-fried, baked, barbecued or poached very briefly; it toughens when overcooked.

Serving Suggestions

Serve on canapés as starters, in salads, soups, casseroles and sauces; sauté in flavored oils; or coat in egg and bread crumbs and deep-fry. Use in any recipe calling for clams.

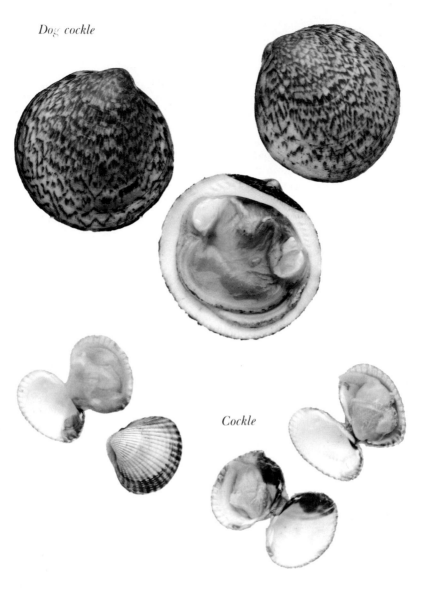

Dog cockle

Cockle

Limpet

Limpets *(Patella vulgata)* are not normally eaten these days. They are rarely seen on sale at fish markets as they are not commercially marketed. Although they are edible and were once quite popular in Britain, they are not particularly tender or good to eat.

Limpets are usually collected off rocks around the British coastline at low tide; January, February and March are said to be the best months to collect them.

The Scots used to mix limpets with oatmeal before cooking, while along the south coast they were piled up on the rocks and covered with burning straw to cook them.

Limpets are small, usually about 2 inches across, with a grey, yellowish or brown conical shell which is almost symmetrical. The inside of the shell is pearly.

Limpets found off the coast of North America are even smaller and barely worth eating.

Preparation

To clean, soak limpets in a bucket of lightly salted water for 2 to 3 hours, then boil for about 10 minutes. They can also be eaten raw or baked briefly with a little butter.

Limpets are probably best used to flavor sauces.

Periwinkle

The periwinkle *(Littorina littorea)*, or winkle as it is also known, has a small snail-like shell about 1 inch long. The convoluted shell is usually dark grey or brown.

Like cockles and whelks, periwinkles are traditionally sold ready cooked from street stalls in London and on seaside promenades. They are usually sold cold, dressed in vinegar. These stalls are a less common sight these days.

Periwinkles were formerly popular in Northern Ireland where they were called willicks. They were usually extracted from their shells with a pin (called a periwinkle pick) and dipped in oatmeal before eating.

Periwinkles have been popular in Europe for centuries and are still often found in the *fruits de mer* platter of coastal towns of Brittany.

Buying & Storing

Periwinkles are harvested commercially. They are usually sold cooked. If bought uncooked, soak for 1 hour in salted water with a sprinkling of oatmeal or flour to rid them of any grit. Take out the periwinkles, change the water and repeat the process. Cook periwinkles within 24 hours of purchase.

Preparation

Boil in their shells in salted water or court bouillon (see page 24) for about 5 minutes. Serve in the shell: each diner removes the meat with a seafood pick and seasons it with salt, pepper and vinegar.

Serving Suggestions

Serve as part of a seafood platter for starters or buffets, or as a tasty snack.

Periwinkle

Whelk

Whelk

The whelk *(Buccinum undatum)* resembles the periwinkle as it has a similar snail-like shell, but the whelk is much larger. Whelks often reach 4 inches in length; some are as long as 6 inches. American whelks are even larger; *Busycon carica*, for example, can reach 12 inches.

The shell of the whelk varies in color from grey to brown and is often striped. Its lips have great powers of suction and are used to kill other mollusks, sucking out their contents. It is the large, muscular foot which is normally eaten, although they can be eaten whole.

Buying & Storing

Whelks are commercially harvested, and this is certainly the best way to obtain them. They are usually sold cooked and removed from their shells.

If bought uncooked, soak for 1 hour in salted water with a sprinkling of oatmeal or flour. Change the water and soak again. This purges them of their dirt. Cook as soon as possible, certainly within 24 hours of purchase.

Preparation

Boil uncooked whelks in shells in salted water or court bouillon (see page 24) for about 5 minutes. Remove from their shells with a skewer or fork and dress with salt, pepper and vinegar.

Serving Suggestions

Serve whelks as part of a seafood platter for starters or buffets; marinate in herb dressing and serve with brown bread and butter; bake with garlic butter in the same way as you would snails; add them to omelets and rice dishes.

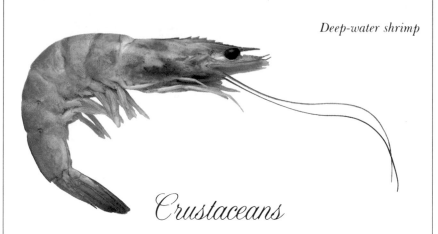

Deep-water shrimp

Crustaceans

Crustaceans are shellfish which have an external skeleton. They all have legs and are able to move. Some, like lobsters, have a jointed shell which helps them to move. Crab do not have a jointed shell but use their legs to scurry about.

Crustaceans are members of the *Arthropoda* family which includes spiders, scorpions and insects. They are covered in a hard horny shell or, more correctly, carapace. This shell is shed periodically as the creature grows—evidence of which can be seen washed up on shorelines. Generally speaking it is a good idea to choose lobsters and crab whose shells are encrusted and obviously old as the flesh will have had time to develop and fill the shell. A crustacean with a new shell will often be small and lacking in flavor. An exception to this rule is the soft-shell crab (see page 40).

Crustaceans range from the tiniest shrimp with its semitransparent fragile shell, to the large lobster whose tough shell can often be utilized as a serving dish. Their flesh is firm and sweet, particularly the fine flavored lobster and the delicate freshwater crayfish.

Many crustaceans are available all year, but tend to be at their best in the summer. When choosing a large crustacean such as lobster or crab, look for specimens which feel heavy for their size, with legs and claws intact. Ideally, they should be bought live, but if already cooked store in the refrigerator and eat as soon as possible—certainly within 24 hours.

Most shellfish have indigestible or inedible parts, such as the gills or 'dead men's fingers' of crab and lobsters, or the intestinal tract of the large shrimp. These must be removed during preparation. The roe, also called coral, and liver, sometimes called tomalley, of the lobster should never be discarded. They are considered delicacies and can be used to make delicate sauces.

The cooking time for all crustaceans tends to be short as the flesh is tender and can become dry very quickly with overcooking. Many change their color when cooked: the blue-black lobster turns scarlet and the blue-grey shrimp turns pink. Lobsters are usually boiled in salt water or a court bouillon (see below), then served plain or with a sauce.

Small crustaceans such as shrimp can be deep-fried; they are usually first coated in batter or egg and bread crumbs to protect their delicate flesh from the heat. They can also be broiled, either marinated first or brushed with butter or oil to keep them moist.

The tiny, superbly flavored, brown shrimp is eaten boiled with sauce or in salads.

Court Bouillon
To a large pan of cold water, add 1/4 bottle white wine or wine vinegar, 1 sliced carrot, 1 sliced onion, 1 sliced celery stalk, 12 peppercorns, 2 bay leaves, 3 parsley sprigs and a little salt. Simmer for 20 minutes before adding the shellfish.

Selection of crustaceans: crab, lobster, Dublin Bay prawn (langostino), scampi tail, crab claw, king prawn, pink shrimp and brown shrimp

Shrimp

Shrimp are probably the most well known and popular seafood. They are called prawns in Britain. There are two main categories: the common shrimp *(Palaemom serratus)* of the *Palaemonidae* family, and the deep-water or Northern shrimp *(Pandalus borealis)* of the *Pandalidae* family. There are several related species which are rarely distinguised from each other.

The common shrimp is found in shallow inshore waters. It walks forward, looking for food with its antennae and sweeping the seabed with its second pair of legs. It is fished extensively from Norway down to the Mediterranean. It reaches a maximum length of 3-1/2 inches and when alive its shell is almost colorless.

The deep-water shrimp is larger with a maximum length of 5 inches. This shrimp is red when alive and is usually cooked at sea, before it reaches the market. Its range extends from Greenland to Britain, with large quantities caught along the Norwegian coast.

Large shrimp called king prawns belong to the *Penaeidae* family and include the Mediterranean shrimp fished off Spain and Portugal. There are also several varieties found in Australia. King prawns can reach lengths of up to 8 inches. They are usually blue-grey and have succulent meaty flesh. They make good starters, particularly when bought raw and freshly cooked. The most commonly found king prawns are: the *Parapenaeus longirostris,* called the *crevette rose* in France because of its pink color, which has a maximum length of 6 inches; *Penaeus kerathurus,* brown with reddish tints, often called *crevette royale* in France, is a little larger, up to 9 inches and *Aristeus antennatus (crevette rouge* in France), which has a light red body and mauve head and is up to 8 inches long. All these species are found in the waters of the Mediterranean.

Other common types include the Eastern shrimp *(Penaeus plebegus),* Western shrimp *(Penaeus latisulcatus),* creamy yellow banana shrimp *(Penaeus merguiensis),* and the brown tiger shrimp *(Penaeus esculentus),* so called because of its brown and orange striped shell.

In Australia you will find another group of shrimp. Two which fall somewhere in size between a deep-water and a king prawn are the school shrimp *(Metapenaeus macleayi),* found in rivers and bays, and the greentail shrimp *(Metapenaeus bennettae)* which is caught mainly in estuaries.

In Britain, the term shrimp describes only the brown shrimp *(Crangon crangon)* which, with a maximum length of just 2-1/2 inches, is one of the smallest crustaceans to be eaten in any quantity. This translucent little creature lives on sandy sea bottoms and can vary its color from grey to brown to match its surroundings and provide camouflage.

Shrimp commonly found in the United States: the American brown shrimp *(Penaeus aztecus aztecus),* pink shrimp *(Penaeus duorarum duorarum)* and white shrimp *(Penaeus setiferus)* are much larger. They can vary in size from 2 to 6 inches and are more closely related to the king prawn. They are fished south of the Carolinas and along the Gulf Coast. Much of the shrimp eaten in the United States is from the Mexican coast.

Buying & Storing

Shrimp are available all year around. Shrimp are sold raw (dead, but uncooked) or cooked, shelled or unshelled, whole or headless. Raw shrimp should have a firm body, without black traces, and a fresh sea smell. Cooked shrimp should have firm flesh with tight shells and no black or loose heads or legs.

Shrimp are best eaten on the day of purchase and peeled just before serving to retain moisture. Store in an airtight container in the refrigerator, but eat within 24 hours.

Preparation

To cook raw shrimp, plunge them into boiling salted water and simmer for 3 to 5 minutes, until they have turned pink; large shrimp will take 6 to 8 minutes.

To peel shrimp, break or cut off the head, then slip off the tail and body shell. Slit large shrimp down the

Deep-water shrimp

Common shrimp

Brown tiger shrimp

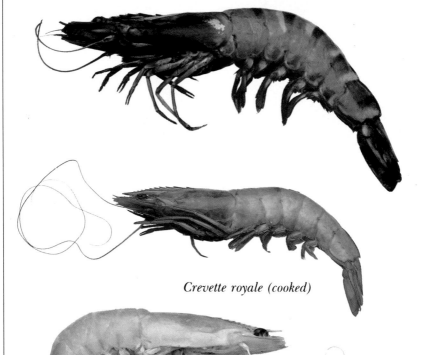

Crevette royale (cooked)

Banana shrimp (raw)

King prawn—Penaeidae (cooked)

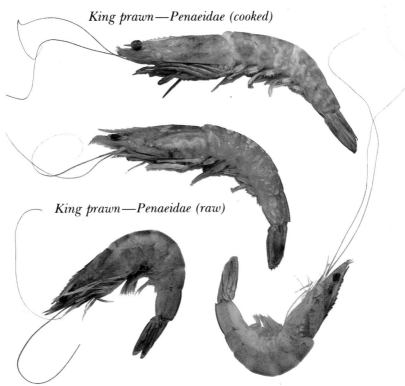

King prawn—Penaeidae (raw)

Western shrimp (raw)

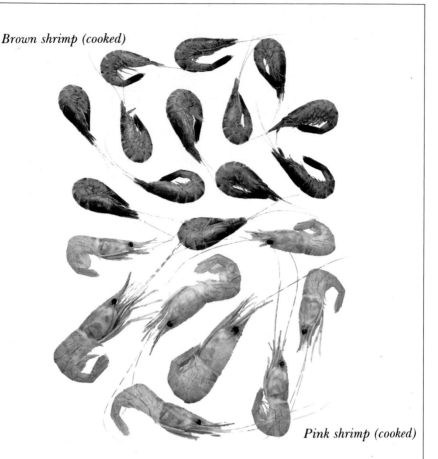

Brown shrimp (cooked)

Pink shrimp (cooked)

center back with a small sharp knife, then carefully remove the dark intestinal vein. The end of the tail section is often left on, particularly when the shrimp are to be broiled or barbecued. The tail is usually removed from smaller shrimp.

Serving Suggestions
Shrimp can be broiled, stir-fried, deep-fried or baked. Cooked shrimp are useful in salads, shrimp cocktails and countless starter and main course dishes: shrimp risotto, Shrimp Satay (page 75), Spicy Chinese Shrimp (page 74) and shrimp kabobs are just a few examples. When using cooked shrimp in a hot dish, reheat carefully to avoid them becoming tough.

Serve cold, cooked shrimp in their shells as a starter. Dip into warm lemon butter or a spicy horseradish and tomato sauce. Provide finger bowls or lots of napkins and serve with thinly sliced brown bread and butter.

The flavor of small shrimp is excellent and makes a particularly good addition to creamy rice or pasta dishes; stuffings for fish fillets, such as sole or plaice; or little molds to serve as starters.

Dublin Bay Prawn

The Dublin Bay prawn *(Nephrops norvegicus)* is also called Norway lobster or Icelandic lobster. It is the same species as the *langoustine*, featured on so many French seaside menus, and the *scampi* in Italy, so often battered or egg-and-crumbed and frozen. They are often called langostinos in America.

This crustacean is rose-grey or pink in color and can reach up to 10 inches in length. It is found most commonly in the Adriatic and west and central parts of the Mediterranean.

Dublin Bay prawns are so called not because they are caught in the bay, but because fishing boats often came into Dublin Bay having caught the shellfish accidentally along with their catch. They would then sell them off the boats to Dublin street vendors.

Buying & Storing
In the Mediterranean, Dublin Bay prawns are usually sold in their shells, live or cooked. In Britain and America they are more commonly sold as frozen tails, but are becoming more widely available whole, either live or cooked.

They are often sold as scampi, though correctly this name should be used only for the large shrimp from the Bay of Naples. Scampi is available cooked or frozen raw.

Live Dublin Bay prawns should be evenly colored with no black discoloration. Look for a firm body and pleasant sea smell.

Cooked Dublin Bay prawns should have firm flesh, no missing or black limbs and a pleasant sea smell. Leave in the shell until needed as this keeps the flesh succulent. Store in the refrigerator and eat within 24 hours of purchase.

Preparation
Cook live Dublin Bay prawns in boiling salted water for 10 to 12 minutes, depending on size.

To shell, twist off the head then gently pull off the tail shell and remove the body shell. Cut down the back and remove the dark vein.

Serving Suggestions
These shellfish can be eaten hot or cold. They are often served as a starter, cold with mayonnaise or hot with melted butter or warm hollandaise sauce.

They may be coated in egg and bread crumbs and deep-fried, or cooked in a wine sauce to serve with rice. They are particularly good with spicy sauces, such as sweet and sour or creole sauce.

Mantis Shrimp

This unusual looking creature is related to the crab, but looks much more like a shrimp. It grows to a maximum length of 10 inches and has a yellowish-green shell. It has five pairs of legs; the front pair serve as extensions to the mouth and the next pair are used to grasp food. This action resembles that of the praying mantis, hence its name.

The mantis shrimp *(Squilla empusa)* is found in mud holes around the eastern seaboard of the United States. Its European relative *Squilla mantis* is brown-grey in color and is mainly found in the waters of Spain, France and Portugal.

Mantis shrimp are rarely available in European and American markets, except around the Mediterranean.

Preparation & Serving
In the Mediterranean region, mantis shrimp are often used in fish soups and stocks. Or they may be boiled or steamed and then shelled and eaten like shrimp.

Dublin Bay prawn (cooked)
(langostino)

Lobster

The European lobster (*Homarus gammarus*) and the American lobster (*Homarus americanus*) are similar in appearance, but the American is larger. The European lobster is found from the far north to the Mediterranean. The American lobster is found as far south as South Carolina.

Lobsters can only be caught in special lobster pots and this is one of the reasons for their cost. They are available throughout the year but are at their best during the summer.

As with other crustaceans, a lobster will shed its shell periodically as it grows. The lobster is not good to eat immediately after moulting a shell as it absorbs a large amount of water to help it fit into its new shell; the flesh is therefore watery and tasteless. A more mature shell with be thick and encrusted and the creature will feel heavy for its size.

The female lobster has the more tender flesh. The coral-colored roe under its tail can be cooked separately and used to make lobster butter or added to sauces to impart a delicate flavor.

Buying & Storing

Lobsters are available live or cooked. Live lobsters should be active, with intact legs. Do not buy a dead uncooked lobster, unless you are certain it has just been killed, as it deteriorates quickly.

When buying cooked lobsters look for intact legs and bright eyes. They should be heavy for their size and there should be no discoloration at the joints.

Wrap cooked lobster in foil and store in the refrigerator for up to 2 days.

Preparation

Live lobsters are normally sold with their claws banded. If not, secure the large claws with rubber bands. Put lobsters, head down, in a large pan of fast boiling well-salted water or court bouillon (see page 24). Cover and bring to a boil, then simmer, allowing 12 minutes for a 1-pound lobster; 20 minutes for a 2-pound one. For larger lobsters, allow an extra 5 minutes for every additional pound.

In recipes where a live lobster is not boiled first but broiled, ensure the claws are held with rubber bands. Hold underside down on a board, then place the point of a strong knife on the shell at the place where the body and tail meet and plunge it quickly down through the body.

To split a freshly killed lobster for broiling or lobster thermidor, using a sharp knife, cut firmly from the upper body down towards the tail, splitting the tail in two. Save the coral, if any, and the yellow-green liver, which is delicious added to sauces. Discard the stomach sac near the eyes and the intestine, which is the dark thread-like membrane running down the body.

To broil, use a sharp knife to slit the underside several times to help heat penetration. Brush with oil or melted butter and broil for 12 to 15 minutes, turning once.

A cooked lobster is split and prepared in the same way. To extract the meat, snap off legs and break each apart at the joint. Remove flesh with a skewer. Snap each claw free near the body, then crack the claw shells with a mallet or a lobster cracker; remove meat in one piece, if possible. With lobster on its back, cut down either side of the shell, then pull away the bony covering which protects the underside. Starting at the tail end, remove the flesh in one piece.

Serving Suggestions

Good quality lobsters are very good freshly boiled, split in half and served with lemon or lime juice and a sprinkling of pepper. Sauces that go well with lobster include mayonnaise, plain or flavored with herbs, paprika or garlic; hollandaise; thick sour cream and dill; or tomato and wine. A butter sauce flavored with the mashed coral is an excellent accompaniment for broiled lobster.

European lobster (uncooked)

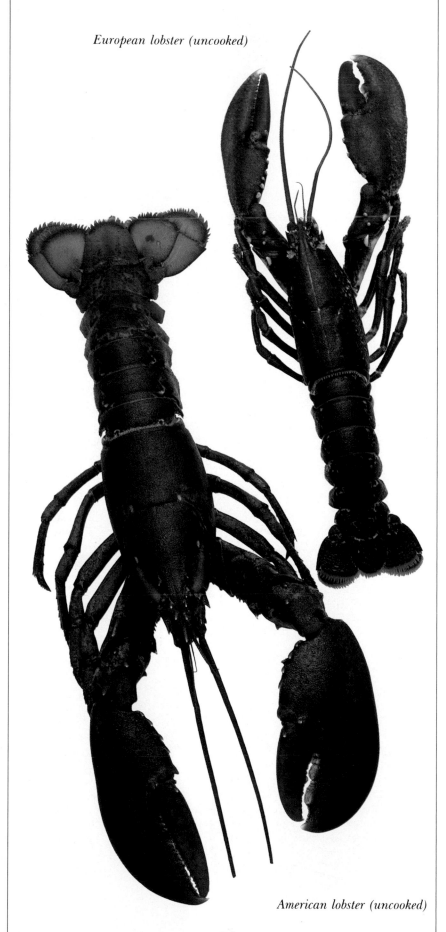

American lobster (uncooked)

American lobster (cooked)

European lobster (cooked)

Spiny lobster tail (cooked)

Spiny lobster tail (uncooked)

Spiny Lobster

The main difference between the spiny lobster and the true lobster is that the spiny lobster *(Palinuras elephas, var. vulgaris)* does not have the huge claws of the true lobster. The flesh is comparable in quality and they lend themselves to the same dishes. The smaller the species, the more tender the flesh. They reach a maximum length of 20 inches but can be much smaller.

Spiny lobsters are found around the waters of Britain and the Mediterranean. They are reddish-brown with yellow and white markings. Spiny lobsters around European waters are becoming a rare catch, so prices are high when they are available.

Australian saltwater crayfish are strictly speaking spiny lobsters. Fishing for them in the waters of Southern Australia is a thriving industry. Most are exported to the United States, because of American marketing laws they are called rock lobsters *(Panulirus* and *Jasus).*

To confuse matters further, the spiny lobster is often referred to as crawfish or crayfish, although it should be termed saltwater crayfish, as it is quite different from the small freshwater crayfish (see page 46).

The Western rock lobster *(Panulirus cygnus)* varies in color from pink to reddish-brown and maroon. It is found in Western Australia and is excellent eating.

The Southern rock lobster *(Jasus novaelollandiae)* is yellow, orange or purple, while the Eastern rock lobster *(Jasus verreauxii)* is olive-green.

Buying & Storing

Whole spiny lobsters are available live or cooked. These lobsters are however more commonly sold as lobster tail—uncooked or cooked.

When bought live, spiny lobsters should have all their legs and be active. Do not buy a dead uncooked whole spiny lobster, as the flesh deteriorates quickly.

When buying cooked whole spiny lobsters, again the legs should be intact, the eyes bright and there should be no discoloration at the joints. The crustacean should be heavy in weight in proportion to its size.

Spiny lobster (cooked)

Preparation

Put live, spiny lobsters in a large pan of boiling water, bring to a boil, then boil for 8 minutes per pound.

To broil uncooked tails, slit the underside of the tail a couple of times to allow for heat penetration, then brush with oil or butter and broil for 5 to 8 minutes on each side.

To cook frozen spiny lobster tails, thaw in refrigerator before cooking.

To remove the meat from a whole spiny lobster, first break off the claws and legs. Crack the large claws with a lobster cracker or mallet and remove the meat with a skewer.

Twist off the head from the tail. Use kitchen scissors to cut away the thin underside of the tail shell. Gently pull the meat out. Cut along the back of the meat to a depth of 1/4 inch and discard the dark vein. Reserve the red coral, if any, to make lobster butter or to add flavor to a savory sauce. Add the greenish liver to the lobster meat.

Lift out the bony portion from the head shell and pick out any further pieces of coral or liver. Use a lobster pick or the point of a knife to pick the meat from the head. Discard the stomach sac and greyish spongy gills from the top of the head.

Break the bony portion in several pieces and remove the meat with a pick or fork.

Serving Suggestions

Serve warm spiny lobster tails plain with a little lime or lemon juice, with mayonnaise, thick sour cream and herbs, or a rich wine and tomato sauce.

To serve in the half shell, lay the cooked spiny lobster on its back and, using a sharp knife, split from the center to the end of the tail, then from the center to the head. Cut through the flesh and split open. Rinse thoroughly, discarding inedible parts described above.

Flat Lobster

The flat or slipper lobster (*Scyllarus arctus*) has a flat slipper-shaped shell and no claws. It is a small lobster found in the Mediterranean which grows to a maximum length of 5 inches. The tail meat of the flat lobster has a good flavor but unfortunately there is not much of it, so this crustacean is more often than not relegated to the soup pot.

A larger related species of slipper lobster (*Scyllarides squammosis*) is found off the coast of southern Queensland in Australia and makes good eating. The American species is rarely eaten.

Sand Lobster & Bay Bug

Sand lobsters and bay bugs are small lobster-like crustaceans which have similar quality meat. These include the shovel-nosed lobster (*Scyllaridae*), also called sand lobster or bay lobster, and bay bugs which have no claws, a flattened body and broad antennae. Sand lobsters are sometimes called rudder-nosed lobsters because of their ability to flip backwards and steer themselves with their antennae. They are similar to flat or slipper lobsters and both species make cricket-like noises in the water.

The Moreton Bay bug (*Thenus orientalis*) and Balmain bug (*Ibacus*) are species of sand lobster caught commercially in the coastal waters and bay of southeastern Australia.

Sand lobster tails (uncooked)

Rock lobster tails (uncooked)

Bay bugs (cooked)

Flat (or Slipper) lobster tails (cooked)

Crab

Crab are available all year around, but are at their best during the summer. They are one of the choicest shellfish and are readily available either live or cooked. Most crab are encased in a hard, rigid shell which must be shed at intervals to allow growth. In the first year of a crab's life, moulting is very frequent, but after that growth slows down. In Britain it is illegal to sell crab that are not fully grown—less than 5 inches across—or if they are females carrying eggs.

The common crab *(Cancer pagurus)* is a large crab—up to 8 inches across—found in Britain and Europe. It is found as far north as Norway, but does not occur on the American side of the Atlantic.

The rock crab *(Cancer irroratus)* has a yellowish back dotted with brown or purple spots, measuring up to 4 inches. It is found from Labrador to Florida and is a close relative to the Jonah crab *(Cancer borealis)*. The Jonah crab has a brick-red shell and is a little larger, weighing about 1 pound. These crab do not have the fine flavor of many of the others but are well worth eating.

The blue crab *(Callimectes sapidus)*, also known as blue manna or sand crab, has a mottled blue body and legs. It is mainly found in North American waters, but has been introduced to the eastern Mediterranean where it has colonized. It is very popular in America and fishing for it extends from Delaware Bay to Florida and the Gulf States. Chesapeake Bay has the biggest catch, around 200 million per year, which is enough to meet the demands of the whole nation. An agile and fast swimming crab, it is caught in baited crab traps in bays and harbors.

An excellent quality crab, the meat at the base of the legs and in the long claws is finely textured and very sweet—it is considered by many to be the finest of all crabmeats. They are marketed according to size: whales or slabs are the biggest, at over 5 inches across, then come jumbos, primes, hotels and mediums, which are the smallest.

The mud crab *(Scylla serrata)*, also known as mangrove crab, is found throughout Southeast Asia where it lives in shallow muddy water among the mangroves in creeks and estuaries. Mud crab are also found around the northern Australian coast, from Western Australia to central New South Wales.

Mud crab are dull green, grow to about 4 pounds and are usually sold live. The flesh in the claws is the most prized as it is sweet and succulent. The body meat has a good flavor, but is coarser.

The Southern stone crab *(Menippe mercenaria)* is caught from Texas around to Florida up to the Carolinas, but is regarded by many as belonging to Florida. It lives in deep holes in mud or heaps of rock in tidal creeks and estuaries. It is greyish in color and has huge claws, one larger than the other. Its four pairs of feet have hairy spiked ends. It has a very hard shell and only the claw meat is edible. Stone crab claws are often available.

The small shore or green swimming crab *(Carcinus maenus)* is cultivated in the lagoon of Venice. The meat is not particularly highly flavored and is mainly used for soups and stocks. The shell is green and its maximum width is 2-1/2 inches. The Latin name *maenus* means frenzied, which describes the way the creature fights back when captured. If they are collected after they have shed their old shells but before their new ones have hardened, they can be cooked and eaten whole; such crab are known as *moleche* in Venice, where they are eaten with great enjoyment.

The spider crab *(Maia squinado)* is so called because of its round body and spider-like legs. It is found in many waters, particularly around the Adriatic. The shell is spiny—hence its other name spiny crab—and ranges in color from reddish orange to brown. It hides very successfully in rocks, using seaweed and shore plants to disguise itself.

Common·crab—underside (cooked)

Common crab (cooked)

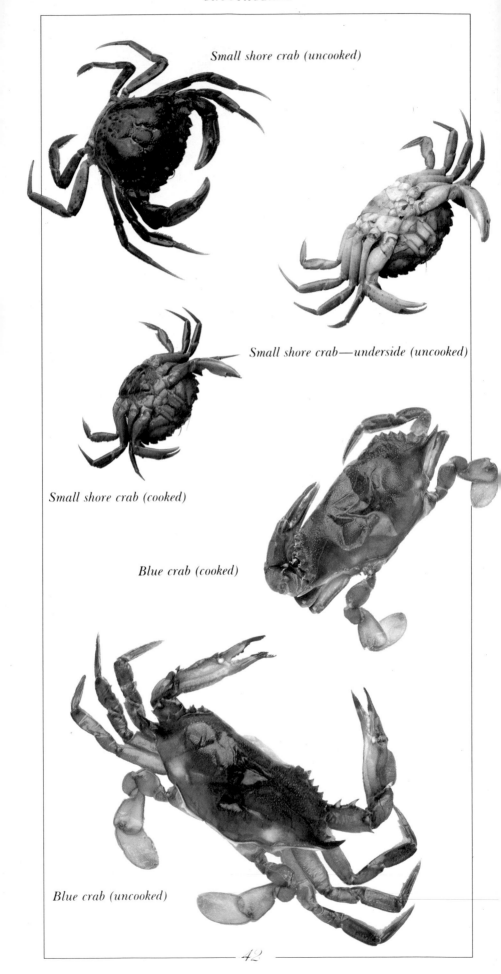

Small shore crab (uncooked)

Small shore crab—underside (uncooked)

Small shore crab (cooked)

Blue crab (cooked)

Blue crab (uncooked)

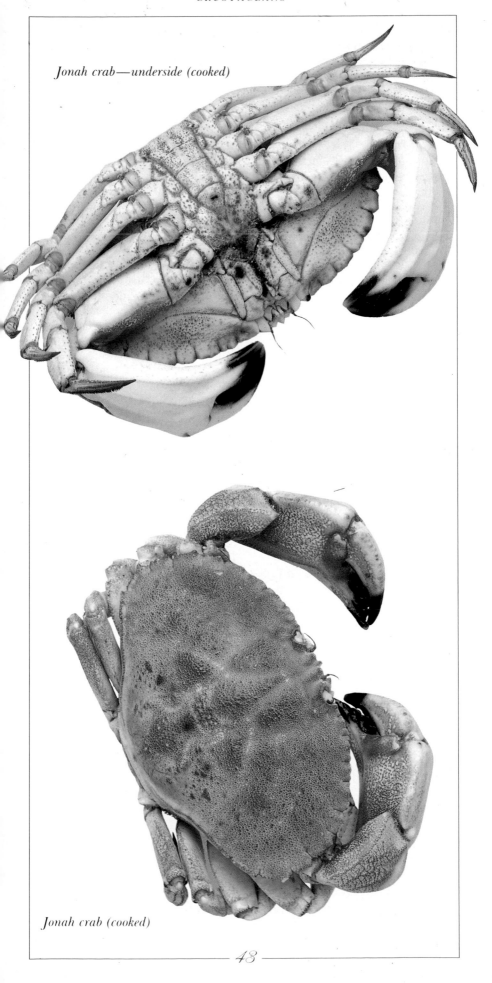

Jonah crab—underside (cooked)

Jonah crab (cooked)

The spider crab has a good flavor and is usually poached and served in its shell.

The red crab (Geryon quinquedens) is bright red and up to 6 inches across. It is a deep sea crab, found at depths of between 100 to 300 feet in seas from Nova Scotia to Cuba. It has a good flavor and although the legs are thin, the meat is easily removed.

The snow crab (Chionoecetes opilio) is found only in cold northerly waters; it is particularly popular in Canada. The claws of the snow crab are long and thin, yielding excellent meat. Another northern crab is Alaskan king crab, which averages 10 pounds. It is usually available frozen.

The spanner crab (Ranina ranina), also known as frog crab, has claws that resemble spanners (wrenches); the shape also appears frog-like. It is found in the sheltered bays and coastal waters of Australia along southern Queensland and northern New South Wales. It is deep red with cream to pale pink tonings, and grows to over 8 inches in length. The meat is white and fine textured. The crab, usually sold cooked, are best cut lengthwise before extracting the meat.

Buying & Storing
Crab are usually sold already cooked. Choose one which has all the legs intact and feels heavy for its size. Lift the crab and shake before buying—there should be no sound of water.

Uncooked crab are best bought live as the meat deteriorates quickly once the creature is dead; look for lively, clean-looking crab.

Store live crab in a damp burlap bag and eat within 24 hours. Wrap cooked crab in foil and store in the refrigerator for 1 to 2 days. Freeze for up to 3 months.

Preparation
If you buy a live crab, kill it humanely before cooking. Place the crab on its back and use a small sharp knife to stab the ventral nerve center under the tail flap, and the point just above the brain between the eyes. Insert the knife several times into each of these points, varying the angle slightly each time. Rinse the crab thoroughly under cold running water to clean.

Place the crab in a pan of cold salted water. Cover and bring slowly to a boil, then boil for 8 to 10 minutes per pound, taking care not to overcook. Leave to cool in the water to help keep the flesh tender and moist.

To extract the meat from a cooked crab, place shell down on a work surface. Twist off the claws and legs. Crack the claws with a mallet to extract the meat. Break apart the legs and remove the meat with a skewer.

Twist the apron free on the underside of the crab and discard. Insert a strong knife between the main shell and underside part where the legs were attached. Pry upwards to detach the underside; set aside.

Scoop out the meat from the main shell, discarding the small greyish-white stomach sac and its appendages, just behind the crab's mouth. Pull away the soft grey feathered gills, known as 'dead men's fingers,' along the edges of the underside and discard. Using a heavy knife, split the underside down the middle, then remove the flesh from the crevices using a skewer.

If the crab is to be served in its shell, break away the shell edge along the natural dark rim; scrub the shell thoroughly.

Serving Suggestions
A good quality crab is excellent eaten freshly boiled with lemon and black pepper, or cold with mayonnaise. For a dressed crab, the brown meat from the body is arranged in the center of the cleaned shell, with the white meat from the claws and legs on either side.

Crab can also be used in countless other dishes; try it broiled (see page 99); combined with vegetables and fruit, such as asparagus (see page 97) or orange (see page 96), to make a tasty salad; as a delicate mousse (see page 98); or as a stuffing for cannelloni or ravioli (see page 100). The meat is sweet and succulent and should not be masked with too many other flavors.

Lesser quality crab are used as a base for soups and stews, or used in crab cakes, sauces and stuffings.

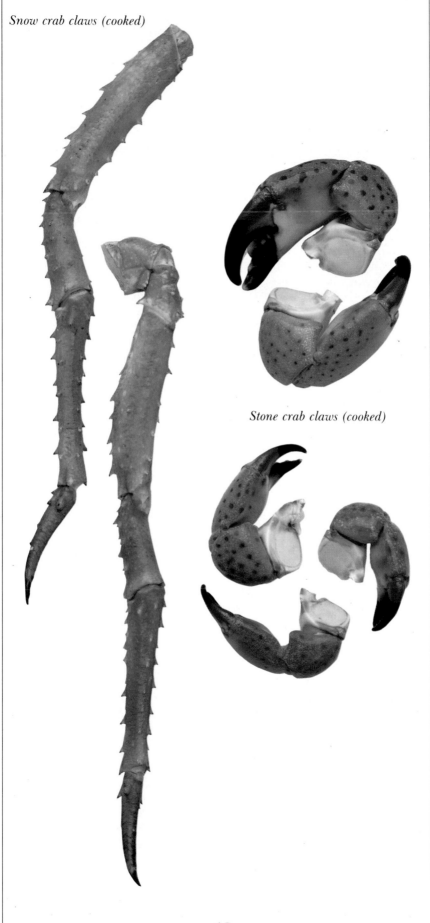

Snow crab claws (cooked)

Stone crab claws (cooked)

Freshwater Crayfish

Freshwater crayfish (*Austropotamobius pallipes*) are prized for their delicate flavor and are well worth eating when available. In Europe and America they tend to be small—about the same size as langostinos—but much larger species are found in Australia. The Tasmanian crayfish (*Astacopsis gouldi*) for example can reach 12 pounds.

Murray River crayfish (*Euastacus armatus*) grow to around 4 pounds and have spiny blue shells. The similar-sized marron (*Cherax tenuimanus*), which comes from freshwater pools around Western Australia, is much flavored for its excellent eating qualities.

The smaller crayfish of Australia, called freshwater yabbies (*Cherax destructor*), are found in rivers, creeks, lakes, dams and billabongs. They are usually brown, but can be green, blue or purple. They are a little larger than the American freshwater crayfish, reaching up to 12 inches in length.

Buying & Storing
Freshwater crayfish can be bought live or cooked. Check that the claws are intact, the shells firm and that they have a pleasant sea smell. Live crayfish should be lively and intact. Store live crayfish for up to 24 hours. Wrap cooked crayfish in foil and store in the refrigerator for up to 2 days.

Preparation
Put live crayfish into a large pan of boiling water and bring to a boil. Reduce heat. Simmer for about 5 minutes, until they turn red all over. Drain and leave until cool enough to handle. To shell crayfish, twist off the head and peel away the shell from the tail.

Serving Suggestions
Freshwater crayfish are a great delicacy and excellent for starters and seafood platters. They look extremely attractive as the central part of a dish or as a garnish. They can form the focal point of a mixed seafood salad on a bed of interesting lettuce leaves, or make a spectacular garnish in their shells beside a plate of poached fish in a creamy sauce. Turbot, salmon and monkfish go very well with crayfish.

Cooked crayfish tails can be simply served on a bed of lettuce with mayonnaise or a vinaigrette dressing.

The cooked shells can be pounded or puréed and used as the basis for a delicious rich sauce to accompany the crayfish tails.

Goose-Necked Barnacle

This creature is quite unlike any other crustacean both in appearance and taste. It consists of a finger-thick tube with a dark dry papery skin covered in tiny scales. On top of this is a pair of white hooflike pads and between these the creature's feet are visible. This unusual crustacean can be up to 6 inches in length.

Goose-necked barnacles (*Pollicipes cornucopia*) are to be found clinging to rocks in groups. They are very popular in Spain and Portugal but as demand is greater than supply their availability is diminishing.

The edible part is inside the tube; to reach it, pinch the outer skin near the hooflike pads and pry it off with your fingers. The stalklike inside is entirely edible, either raw or lightly cooked in salted water.

Crayfish (uncooked)

Crayfish (cooked)

Crayfish tails (cooked)

Squid

Cephalopods

Squid, cuttlefish and octopus are the most well known members of the cephalopod family. They look like translucent bags with heads and tentacles. They are strictly speaking mollusks—it is thought they originally had an external shell—but as their methods of cooking and preparation are so different to other mollusks, they warrant their own section. Cephalopods are very good to eat, but need careful preparation and cooking to realize their full potential.

Cephalopod means head-footed, presumably because the tentacles emerge from the head. Cuttlefish and squid have 10 tentacles and the octopus has eight. They have no true skeleton, although the cuttlefish and squid have an internal bone. In squid this is transparent and quill-like, but the cuttlefish bone is more substantial; it is dried and used as a calcium source for caged birds.

The octopus is the largest of the cephalopods and has two protruding eyes and suckers all along the tentacles. The octopus can change its color and shape at high speed in order to deter predators.

Another protection all cephalopods have is a sac of dark brown or black ink in the body cavity, which the creature can squirt out to form a protective screen so it can escape.

Cephalopods can be caught in nets or traps; the octopus is sometimes speared. However, most of those sold commercially are caught as a byproduct of trawling. In Mediterranean countries cephalopods are much appreciated and they are prepared and cooked with great skill. Not so long ago, however, squid was thought to be fit only for bait. Cuttlefish, usually smaller than squid, have a delicate flavor that is prized in Japanese cooking.

Cephalopods have firm, rather spicy flesh. Octopus needs to be tenderized either by long slow cooking or, for large specimens, by pounding. Smaller octopus can be sliced and shallow- or deep-fried. Squid and cuttlefish are more tender and can be cut up and fried or stewed, or their bodies can be stuffed and braised or baked. Small cuttlefish are very good simply cleaned and fried whole.

Once you are familiar with the parts of the cephalopods, their preparation is relatively simple. However, they are often sold ready cleaned by the fishmonger. The tentacles and fleshy body sac are the only edible parts; the rest is discarded, including the quill-shaped transparent bone of the squid and the white hard cuttlebone of the cuttlefish. The eyes, skin and mouth are also discarded. If the ink sac is to be used in cooking it must be removed from the body intact. The body of the squid and larger cuttlefish is skinned, but the skin of the octopus is not removable.

Selection of cephalopods: sea urchins and squid

Squid

The squid (*Loligo vulgaris*) has a long cylindrical body with fins on either side. The head has large eyes and two tentacles, and eight 'arms' surround the parrot-like beak. Squid are much smaller than octopus, reaching a maximum size of 20 inches. Internally they have a pen-shaped quill, loosely attached to the pouch.

Squid swim strongly near the surface of the water by jet propulsion through their funnels and are very graceful to see; the fins are used for steering. They are almost transparent in the water, making them almost invisible to predators. Like other cephalopods, squid possess sophisticated pigment cells which enable them to change color rapidly. This explains why some have a mottled purplish-brown skin.

Squid are caught by trawling and are fished throughout the world, but particularly around the coasts of Europe. The above species is the one fished around the Mediterranean. A slightly larger species (*Loligo forbesi*) is found in the Atlantic as far south as Britain. Another common American species is *Loligo pealei*. All of these squid are similar in appearance.

Their relative, the flying squid (*Todarodes sagittatus*), is rather different. It can be up to twice the size and has a purple hue. The flying squid has flat broad swimming fins to the rear of its body, eight 'arms' and two much longer tentacles. It does not really fly, but can propel itself out of the water and glide above the surface. It needs long slow cooking to tenderize it.

Buying & Storing

When buying whole squid look for those with firm flesh; the head and tentacles should be intact. Squid should have a pleasant sea smell. If the skin is difficult to remove, it is a sign of staleness. Squid are often sold ready cleaned, either in tubes or sliced into rings. The flesh should be white, without any brown markings.

Preparation

First rinse thoroughly. To prepare squid, hold the head just below the eyes and gently pull away the body pouch; the soft viscera, including the ink sac, will come with it. Discard the viscera of the pouch, carefully retaining the ink sac intact, if required. Pull back the rim of the body pouch to find the quill-shaped pen. Carefully pull it free and discard.

Cut the head from the tentacles just below the eyes; discard the head. Cut out the small round cartilage at the base of the tentacles.

The tentacles will be in one piece. In the center is the beak-like mouth, which should be removed by squeezing with the fingers.

Slip your fingers under the skin of the body pouch and peel off, then cut the edible fins from the body. Rinse the squid thoroughly under cold running water.

Serving Suggestions

Squid are most commonly served deep-fried in rings. To deep-fry, coat the rings in egg and bread crumbs or batter and deep-fry in hot oil for 1 to 2 minutes; serve with a dipping sauce.

Try the body stuffed and baked (see page 106), or sliced with the tentacles and casseroled in a rich tomato sauce (see pages 104 and 105). In the Mediterranean, squid are often stewed in their own ink with tomatoes, garlic and onions for flavor.

Thinly sliced squid rings can also be stir-fried quickly with sliced vegetables, or stewed and added to seafood salads.

Large squid are usually sliced before they are fried, casseroled or stuffed and baked. Small squid are tender enough to be cooked whole; try frying them in oil or butter, adding garlic or herbs to flavor.

Common squid (large and small)

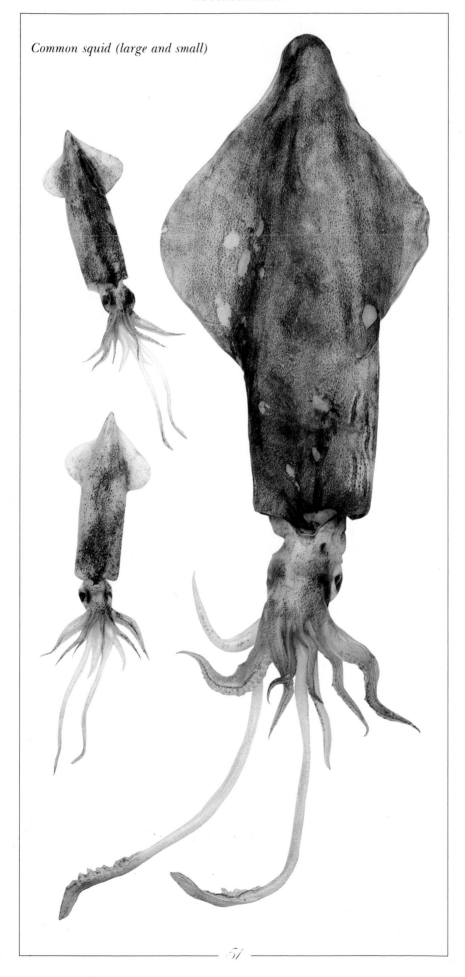

Octopus

The octopus (*Octopus vulgaris*) has a large head with two protruding eyes and eight tentacles, each carrying a twin row of suckers along their length. The body cavity contains a dark brown ink which the creature can squirt to form a screen. This helps to protect it from predators, such as the conger eel. The octopus can also change its color like a chameleon to disguise itself when under attack.

The octopus lives in deep waters in the winter months, swimming nearer to land in early spring and spending the summer in inshore waters. It can be caught in traps, nets and by spearing, but usually those sold in markets are caught by trawling.

An octopus can reach a length of 10 feet, although those normally available for sale are much smaller. Size, however, is no guide to quality—it is the smaller specimens which have the most tender succulent flesh. Large fish need to be beaten to tenderize them before long, slow cooking; it is said they should be beaten one hundred times against a rock!

Two other species worth a mention are the smaller octopus (*Octopus macropus*) and the curled octopus (*Eledone cirrosa*). They are both inferior in quality to the large octopus but can make very good eating if cooked correctly. *Octopus macropus* has a maximum length of 4 feet with long thin elegant tentacles. It is found in warm waters throughout the world. The curled octopus has a maximum length of 16 inches and has curled tentacles each with only a single row of suckers. Both these species are very good cooked in a rich spicy tomato sauce.

Buying & Storing
When buying octopus look for firm resilient flesh with a pleasant sea smell. The larger tougher fish are usually tenderized before being offered for sale. They are also usually sold already cleaned. If not, clean the octopus yourself (as described below) before storing. Store in a container in the refrigerator for up to 24 hours, or freeze for up to 3 months. Only freeze specimens that you know to be absolutely fresh.

Preparation
To prepare octopus, hold the head firmly and, using a sharp knife, cut through the flesh below the eyes, severing the head from the tentacles. Invert the body pouch and remove the intestines and inc sac. Rinse the body pouch well under cold running water. Pick up the tentacles and, with the index finger underneath the center, push the beak up and cut it away.

To tenderize hood and tentacles, if necessary, beat with a meat mallet until they feel soft and have lost their springiness. Remove any scales which may be left in the suckers. An octopus which is less than 4 inches long does not need beating to tenderize.

Plunge the octopus into boiling salted water for 5 minutes; drain well and cool enough to handle.

Using a sharp knife or scissors, cut the tentacles in separate pieces and leave whole or chop, according to the recipe.

Serving Suggestions
Octopus needs tenderizing to make it palatable and long slow braising or stewing is probably the best method. However, the flesh of smaller ones will be tender if cooked very briefly: cut into pieces and stir-fry or deep-fry until tender.

Octopus can be used in Mediterranean-style soups, casseroles such as provençal, cooked in wine (see page 109), served in a spicy coconut sauce (see page 110), in a salad with garlic dressing, in deep-fried seafood dishes or stir-fried with soy sauce and vegetables.

Octopus

Cuttlefish

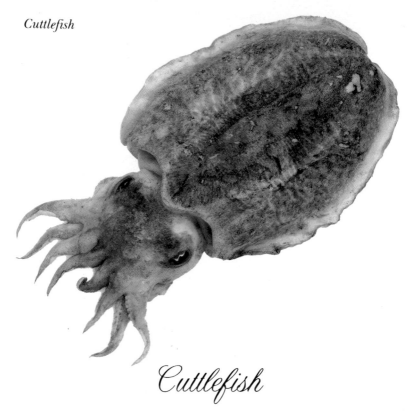

Cuttlefish

The cuttlefish *(Sepia officinalis)* is the smallest member of the cephalopod family. It is oval in shape and can range in length from 1 to 10 inches. The smallest specimens are the sweetest and most tender.

Cuttlefish have eight short tentacles and two much larger ones. The color varies, but there are often mottled or zebra-like markings on the back. Inside the body there is a hard bone which must be removed. Cuttlefish secrete a dark ink which was formerly used to make the color sepia; the Italian name for the fish is *seppia*. Cuttlefish are fished in the eastern Atlantic, the Mediterranean and off the south coast of Britain.

There is a smaller version called Little Cuttlefish *(Sepiola rondeleti)* which has a maximum length of 1-1/2 inches. It has two ear-shaped flaps projecting towards the rear of the body and short tentacles. It is usually cleaned and fried whole.

Buying & Storing

Cuttlefish are available whole and should have clean undamaged bodies with a pleasant sea smell. The flesh should be firm and not discolored. The ink sac is easily broken when it is being caught, but the ink washes off easily.

Cuttlefish should ideally be cooked as soon as possible after purchase. Clean the fish, place in a plastic container and store in the refrigerator for up to 24 hours, or in the freezer for 3 months.

Preparation

To prepare a large cuttlefish, place it bone-side down on a board. Slit the mantle with a sharp knife, open out and remove the gut and cuttlebone; discard. The ink sac, if intact, can be used for cooking. Cut the body in half and remove the skin. The tentacles can be eaten, once the beak is removed, but it is the body which is most commonly used.

Slice the body thinly in rings or sections, or leave it whole for stuffing and baking; score it diagonally before cooking. Chop the tentacles.

Small cuttlefish are usually cleaned and served whole. They are best fried, broiled or barbecued.

Small cuttlefish need only brief cooking as they toughen easily, but large fish need longer cooking to tenderize them.

Serving Suggestions
Broil small cuttlefish with a wine and herb marinade; use them in Chinese stir-fry and steamed dishes, flavored with garlic, ginger and chile; make crisscross cuts across the body to absorb the flavors and cook them in spicy or curry sauces.

Use larger cuttlefish sliced in casseroles or cooked in a sauce—they are particularly good in rich tomato or wine sauces; dip strips or rings in batter and deep-fry; or stuff the body and bake.

Sea Urchin

The sea urchin (*Strongylocentus droebachiensis*) is particularly popular in France and other Mediterranean countries, where they are displayed to great effect in large baskets, in the coastal towns where they are harvested. The edible parts are the star-shaped ovaries, revealed when the creature is cut open.

The sea urchin gets its name from the old English name for hedgehog: urchin. It reaches up to 3 inches in diameter and is caught off the coasts of the Mediterranean; it is also common on the south and west coasts of Ireland.

Buying & Storing
Sea urchins are not generally marketed but are often sold from the beaches and harbors where they are landed. The inside should be fresh and glistening and they should be consumed as soon as possible. They are always sold live as they deteriorate quickly.

Preparation
Cut the sea urchin open horizontally across the middle with scissors, or a special tool called a *coupe-oursin*. The edible parts are the fine orange or pink ovaries which can be clearly seen inside.

Serving Suggestions
The small ovaries are eaten from the shell, sprinkled with a little lemon juice. They can also be added to omelets and scrambled eggs, made into a sauce for poached fish, or used to garnish seafood dishes.

Sea urchin (green)

Sea urchin (purple), cut to reveal edible ovaries

Sea urchin (yellow)

Clam Fritters

4 pounds small clams in shells
1/2 cup dry white wine
1 bay leaf
1 thyme sprig
Vegetable oil for deep-frying
BATTER:
3/4 cup all-purpose flour
Salt and pepper, to taste
1/2 teaspoon paprika
2 eggs, beaten
1 cup milk
TO SERVE:
1 tablespoon grated Parmesan cheese

1. Scrub clams thoroughly under cold running water, scraping off any barnacles. Discard any that are cracked or not tightly closed. Put in a large saucepan with wine, bay leaf and thyme. Cover tightly and steam about 5 minutes, until shells have opened. Drain, discarding any clams that have not opened. Remove clams from shells and chop finely.

2. Sift flour, salt, pepper and paprika into a bowl. Make a well in the center and add eggs. Beat in milk a little at a time until a smooth batter is formed. Stir in clams.

3. In a deep-fryer, heat oil to 350F (175C) or until a 1-inch bread cube browns in 65 seconds. Add spoons of clam mixture, a few at a time, and deep-fry 2 to 3 minutes, until puffy and golden-brown. Drain well on paper towels. Sprinkle with Parmesan cheese and serve with salad, as a light meal or starter.

Makes 4 servings.

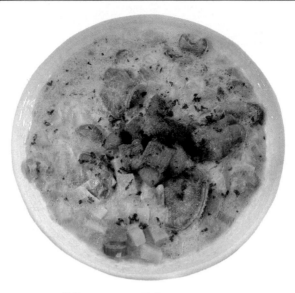

Clam Chowder

3/4 cup dry white wine
2 pounds small clams in shells
2 tablespoons butter
3 bacon slices, diced
2 leeks, shredded
2 celery stalks, thinly sliced
1 pound potatoes, peeled, chopped
1 cup milk
1/2 cup whipping cream
2 tablespoons chopped parsley
Salt and pepper, to taste
TO SERVE:
Garlic Croûtons (see below)

1. Put wine and 1 cup water in a large saucepan. Add clams, cover tightly and cook over high heat 3 to 4 minutes, until shells have opened. Drain, reserving liquid; discard any clams that have not opened. Remove clams from shells and set aside.
2. In a large saucepan, melt butter, add bacon and fry until lightly colored. Add leeks and celery and fry 5 minutes. Add potatoes and strain clam cooking liquid into pan. Bring to a boil, cover and simmer about 20 minutes, until potatoes are tender.
3. Add milk, cream, parsley, clams, salt and pepper and simmer 5 minutes. Serve with Garlic Croûtons, as a light meal.

Makes 4 servings.

Garlic Croûtons: Fry 1/2-inch cubes of crustless white bread in hot oil flavored with a crushed garlic clove until crisp and golden. Drain on paper towels.

Pasta with Clam Sauce

1 red bell pepper
2 cups bread flour
Pinch of salt
2 eggs, beaten
1 tablespoon olive oil
SAUCE:
1/4 cup unsalted butter
1 onion, finely chopped
1 (14-oz.) can chopped tomatoes
Pinch of sugar
Salt and pepper, to taste
1 pound clams in shells, cooked
2 teaspoons chopped tarragon
3 tablespoons chopped parsley

1. Grill bell pepper until evenly charred. Wrap in foil until cool, then remove skin and discard seeds. Purée in a blender or food processor.

Sift flour and salt onto a work surface. Make a well in the center, add eggs, oil and bell pepper purée, then gradually mix in flour mixture to form a soft dough. Knead until smooth.

2. Put the dough through the thin setting of a pasta machine, or roll out as thinly as possible, then roll up like a jellyroll and cut into strips; set aside.

To make sauce, in a pan, melt butter, add onion and fry until softened. Add tomatoes, sugar, salt and pepper and simmer 20 minutes. Purée in a blender or food processor and return to pan.

3. Remove clams from shells and add to sauce with herbs; warm through briefly.

Cook pasta in plenty of boiling salted water 3 to 4 minutes; drain well. Serve the pasta topped with the sauce.

Makes 4 servings.

Note: Use a purchased fresh pasta, flavored with tomato, if preferred.

Variation: Substitute mussels for clams.

Clam Salad with Chile Dressing

1-1/2 pounds clams in shells
Salt and pepper, to taste
4 ounces small green beans
4 ounces button mushrooms
1/2 cup pine nuts
Salad greens
CHILE DRESSING:
1 red chile
1/2 teaspoon fennel seeds
1 tablespoon lemon juice
1/4 cup virgin olive oil
TO GARNISH:
Chervil sprigs

1. Put clams into a saucepan with a little water, salt and pepper. Cover tightly and cook over high heat 2 to 3 minutes, until the shells have opened. Drain and discard any clams that have not opened. Remove clams from shells.

2. To make dressing, wearing rubber gloves, remove stem from chile, halve lengthwise and scrape out seeds; finely chop flesh. Crush fennel seeds and put in a small bowl with chile, lemon juice, oil, salt and pepper. Whisk until thickened.

Blanch beans in boiling salted water 2 minutes; drain and refresh under cold running water.

3. Thinly slice mushrooms. Lightly toast pine nuts. Arrange salad greens on 4 plates. Sprinkle with beans, mushrooms and clams. Drizzle dressing over salads and sprinkle with pine nuts. Garnish with chervil and serve as a light lunch or starter.

Makes 4 servings.

Variation: Substitute mussels for clams.

Mussel Soufflés

1-1/2 pounds mussels in shells
3/4 cup dry white wine
1 garlic clove, crushed
Few saffron strands
Few parsley sprigs
1 bay leaf
Salt and pepper, to taste
2 tablespoons butter
2 teaspoons all-purpose flour
1 tablespoon lemon juice
2 eggs, separated
1/4 cup shredded Gruyère cheese
1 tablespoon grated Parmesan cheese

1. Preheat oven to 350F (175C). Scrub mussels thoroughly under cold running water. Scrape off any barnacles and pull off the beard that protrudes between the shells. Discard any that are open or cracked. Rinse the mussels in a colander.

Put mussels and wine into a saucepan, cover and cook over high heat, shaking pan, about 3 minutes, until shells have opened. Strain, reserving cooking liquid; discard any mussels that have not opened. Remove mussels from shells and set aside.

2. Put cooking liquid, garlic, saffron, parsley, bay leaf, salt and pepper into a pan; boil until reduced to 3/4 cup; strain into a cup. In the same pan, melt butter, add flour and cook 1 minute. Add strained cooking liquid and cook, stirring, until thickened and smooth; stir in lemon juice. Remove from heat and stir some hot mixture into egg yolks; return to pan with cheeses. In a bowl, whisk egg whites until stiff; fold into sauce. Check seasoning.

3. Divide mussels among 4 buttered ramekin dishes. Spoon soufflé mixture over mussels and bake 20 minutes, until puffed and golden-brown. Serve immediately, as a light lunch or starter.

Makes 4 servings.

Mussels with Two Sauces

4 pounds mussels in shells
1/2 cup dry white wine
TOMATO BASIL SAUCE:
1 (14-oz.) can chopped tomatoes
1 tablespoon tomato paste
2 teaspoons torn basil leaves
1 teaspoon chopped fresh oregano
Pinch of sugar
Salt and pepper, to taste
FENNEL SAUCE:
2 tablespoons butter
1 leek, finely chopped
1 fennel bulb, finely chopped
1/4 cup whipping cream

1. Put mussels and wine into a large saucepan, cover and cook over high heat, shaking pan, 4 to 6 minutes, until shells have opened. Drain, discarding any mussels that have not opened; discard the empty half shells. Arrange mussels in their half shells in an ovenproof dish and keep warm.
2. To make Tomato Basil Sauce, put all the ingredients into a saucepan and simmer 15 minutes, until thickened and smooth.

To make Fennel Sauce, in a pan melt butter, add leek and fennel, cover and cook about 5 minutes, until softened. Add cream, season to taste and simmer 2 minutes. Purée in a blender or food processor.
3. Arrange mussels on 4 to 6 plates and fill shells alternately with the two sauces. Serve as a starter or light lunch.

Makes 4 to 6 servings.

Mussels with Pesto

4 pounds mussels in shells
1/2 cup dry white wine
PESTO:
2 ounces basil leaves
2 garlic cloves
1/4 cup pine nuts
Salt and pepper, to taste
1/4 cup grated Parmesan cheese
1/4 cup olive oil
TO FINISH:
1/4 cup dry bread crumbs

1. Preheat oven to 400F (205C). Put mussels and wine into a large saucepan, cover and cook over high heat, shaking pan, 4 to 6 minutes, until shells have opened. Drain, discarding any mussels that have not opened; discard the empty half shells. Set mussels aside.

2. To make Pesto, put basil, garlic, pine nuts, salt and pepper into a mortar, and pound until well blended. (This can be done in a food processor.) Blend in cheese, then add oil a little at a time, until the consistency is thick and creamy.

3. Arrange mussels in their half shells in 4 shallow ovenproof dishes. Spread a little pesto over each and sprinkle with bread crumbs. Bake 10 minutes, until piping hot. Serve immediately, as a starter.

Makes 4 to 6 servings.

Garlic Mussel Puffs

2 pounds mussels in shells
1/2 cup dry white wine
2 tablespoons dairy sour cream
1 garlic clove, crushed
1 tablespoon chopped parsley
1 tablespoon snipped chives
1/4 cup shredded Gruyère cheese
Salt and pepper, to taste
8 ounces puff pastry, thawed
1 beaten egg, to glaze

1. Preheat oven to 425F (220C). Put mussels and wine into a large saucepan, cover and cook over high heat, shaking pan, 3 to 4 minutes until shells have opened; drain, discarding any mussels that have not opened. Remove mussels from shells.

2. Mix together sour cream, garlic, herbs, cheese, salt and pepper. Add mussels and mix well. On a lightly floured surface, roll out pastry thinly and cut out about 40 (2-inch) rounds. Put a mussel and a little sauce on each round, dampen pastry edges and fold in half, sealing well.

3. Place the puffs on a dampened baking sheet and brush with beaten egg. Bake about 10 minutes, until puffed and golden-brown. Serve piping hot, as a starter or snack.

Makes 6 to 8 servings.

Variation: Substitute small clams for mussels.

Mussels in Wine & Cream Sauce

2 cups Muscadet wine
Bouquet garni
6 pounds mussels in shells
2 tablespoons butter
2 shallots, finely chopped
Pinch of turmeric
1/2 cup whipping cream
2 egg yolks
Salt and pepper, to taste
Dash of Tabasco sauce
2 teaspoons chopped fresh tarragon

  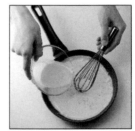

1. Put wine and bouquet garni into a large saucepan. Add mussels, cover and cook over high heat, shaking pan, 5 to 6 minutes, until shells open. Remove mussels with a slotted spoon and discard any that have not opened. Remove mussels from shells and set aside. Boil cooking liquid until reduced by half.

2. In another pan, melt butter; add shallots and fry gently until softened. Stir in reduced liquid and boil until reduced again by one-third. Strain and return to pan with turmeric and all but 1 tablespoon cream; simmer 1 minute.

3. Blend egg yolks with remaining cream and whisk in a little of the hot liquid. Whisk this slowly into pan and heat gently, without boiling, until thickened and smooth. Season with salt, pepper and Tabasco sauce. Add mussels and warm through. Sprinkle with tarragon to serve.

Makes 4 servings.

Oysters Rockefeller

8 ounces spinach leaves
4 bacon slices
1/2 cup butter
3 green onions, finely chopped
2 tablespoons chopped celery leaves
2 tablespoons chopped parsley
1/2 cup dry bread crumbs
1 tablespoon grated Parmesan cheese
1 tablespoon Pernod
24 large oysters, cleaned
Coarse sea salt

1. Preheat oven to 425F (220C). Cook spinach with just the water clinging to the leaves after washing 3 to 4 minutes, until wilted; drain well and chop finely. Broil bacon until crisp, then chop finely. In a saucepan, melt butter; stir in green onions, celery leaves, parsley, spinach, bacon, bread crumbs and cheese. Stir in Pernod. Set aside.

2. To open each oyster, hold in paper towels on a work surface, flatter shell uppermost and hinged end towards you. Insert the point of an oyster knife into the gap in the hinge linking the shells and twist the blade to snap shells apart.

Slide blade along the inside of the upper shell to sever the muscle. Remove any broken shell from the oyster with the point of the knife. Discard empty half shells.

3. Cover the centers of 4 ovenproof plates with sea salt. Set the oysters in their half shells in the salt. Spoon prepared stuffing over oysters and bake 6 to 8 minutes, until bubbling. Serve immediately, as a starter.

Makes 4 servings.

Oysters with Caviar & "Seaweed"

24 large oysters, cleaned
12 quail eggs
4 ounces crème fraîche
1 tablespoon snipped chives
2 ounces caviar
SEAWEED:
1 pound green cabbage
Vegetable oil for deep-frying
1 teaspoon sugar
Salt, to taste

1. Open oysters and discard flatter top shells. Boil quail eggs 1 minute, drain, cool and shell. Mix together crème fraîche and chives.

2. To make "seaweed," shred cabbage by rolling up leaves tightly and slicing thinly with a sharp knife. Heat oil to 350F (175C) or until a 1-inch bread cube turns golden brown in 65 seconds. Add a handful of cabbage, taking care as the oil will pop, count to 10, then remove with a slotted spoon. Drain well on paper towels. Repeat with remaining cabbage. Sprinkle with sugar and salt.

3. Arrange "seaweed" on 4 plates. Place 6 oysters on each plate. On each oyster place a halved quail egg, a spoonful of crème fraîche and a little caviar. Serve hot, as a starter.

Makes 4 servings.

Champagne Oysters

48 oysters, cleaned
1/2 cup butter
2 tablespoons finely chopped green onion
2 teaspoons chopped fresh tarragon
1 teaspoon chopped fresh mint
1-1/2 cups champagne
Salt and pepper, to taste
TO GARNISH:
Mint sprigs
TO SERVE:
Toast

1. To open oysters, hold with paper towels on a work surface, flatter shell uppermost and hinged end towards you. Insert the point of an oyster knife into the gap in the hinge and twist the blade to snap shells apart. Slide blade along the inside of the upper shell to sever the muscle. Discard empty half shells. Remove any broken shell from the oyster with the point of the knife. Remove oysters from shells and set aside. Arrange shells in a circle on 4 plates.
2. In a saucepan, melt 2 tablespoons of the butter; add green onion, tarragon and chopped mint and cook 1 minute. Add champagne and salt and pepper, bring to a boil, then simmer until liquid is reduced by half. Whisk in remaining butter a piece at a time, until sauce is thickened and creamy.
3. Add oysters to sauce and cook gently 2 minutes. Spoon oysters back into shells, covering each with a little sauce. Garnish with mint sprigs and serve with toast, as a starter.

Makes 4 servings.

Scallops with Saffron Sauce

12 to 16 sea scallops in shells
3 tablespoons butter
1 small onion, finely chopped
2 tablespoons dry vermouth
1/2 cup dry white wine
2 tomatoes, peeled, seeded and chopped
1/4 teaspoon powdered saffron
4 ounces small asparagus tips
3 tablespoons crème fraîche
Salt and pepper, to taste

1. First open scallop shells. Holding scallop in a cloth with flat shell uppermost, insert small knife into the small opening between shells. Work blade across inside of flat shell to sever internal muscle. Pry shells apart.
2. Carefully loosen scallops from shells, rinse, removing any dark strands, and pat dry on paper towels.
3. In a skillet, melt half the butter and quickly fry scallops 2 to 3 minutes, until they turn opaque. Remove from pan with any juices and keep warm.

In the same pan, melt remaining butter, add onion and fry about 5 minutes, until softened. Add vermouth, wine, tomatoes and saffron; bring to a boil, then simmer until liquid has reduced by half.

Meanwhile, lightly steam asparagus 3 to 4 minutes until crisp-tender; add to pan with scallops, crème fraîche, salt and pepper. Simmer 2 minutes; check seasoning. Serve with steamed new potatoes or pasta.

Makes 4 servings.

Note: If buying shelled scallops, use 1-1/2 pounds.

Variation: Serve in the cleaned shells, with toast, as a starter for 6 to 8.

Scallop Mousselines

1 pound shelled sea scallops
1/3 cup dry vermouth
2 tablespoons lemon juice
1/2 cup whipping cream
2 egg yolks
Salt and pepper, to taste
SAUCE:
1/3 cup dry vermouth
1/2 cup whipping cream
2 tablespoons unsalted butter
2 teaspoons chopped fresh tarragon
Pinch of paprika

1. Preheat oven to 350F (175C). Rinse scallops, removing any dark strands, and pat dry with paper towels; remove the corals, if present, and set aside. In a large pan, heat vermouth and lemon juice, add scallops and simmer 1 minute; remove with a slotted spoon, reserving liquid, and put into a blender. Heat cream until lukewarm. Blend scallops until smooth; add reserved cooking liquid, egg yolks and cream; blend a few seconds. Season with salt and pepper. **2.** Spoon mixture into 4 buttered ramekin dishes, put into a roasting pan half-filled with hot water and bake 15 to 20 minutes, until firm to the touch.

3. Meanwhile, make sauce. Boil vermouth in a small saucepan until reduced by half. Add cream and again reduce by half. Keeping sauce at a simmer, add half the butter in small pieces, season with salt and pepper and stir in tarragon.

In a small pan, melt remaining butter, add reserved corals and cook 1 to 2 minutes.

Turn the mousselines out onto 4 warmed plates. Top with the sauce, sprinkle with paprika and garnish with corals. Serve immediately, as a starter.

Makes 4 servings.

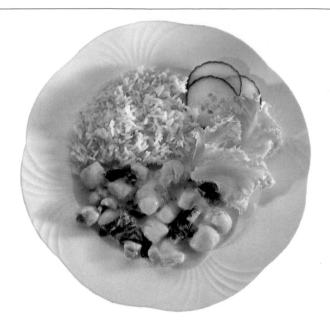

Scallops & Spinach Chardonnay

6 ounces young spinach leaves
Salt, to taste
6 tablespoons butter
1 small onion, finely chopped
2 parsley sprigs
1/2 cup white Chardonnay wine
1/2 cup fish stock
6 black peppercorns
1/4 cup whipping cream
1 to 1-1/2 pounds shelled bay scallops

1. Put spinach into a pan with just the water clinging to the leaves after washing and add a pinch of salt. Cover and cook 3 to 4 minutes, until the leaves have just wilted. Drain and refresh under cold running water. Press out as much water as possible from the leaves. Set aside.

2. In a saucepan, melt 2 tablespoons butter, add onion and fry until softened but not browned. Add parsley, wine, stock and peppercorns. Bring to a boil, reduce heat, then simmer until reduced by two-thirds. Strain and return to pan with cream. Keeping sauce at a gentle simmer, add remaining butter a small piece at a time, stirring with each addition, until sauce is smooth and shiny.

3. Rinse scallops, removing any dark strands, and pat dry with paper towels. Add to pan, cover and cook about 4 minutes, until just cooked. Stir in spinach and heat through. Taste and add salt if necessary. Serve with saffron rice and a crisp salad.

Makes 4 servings.

Poached Scallops in a Nest

4 ounces small green beans
4 small carrots
4 small zucchini
1 pound shelled sea scallops
2 tablespoons lemon juice
6 tablespoons dry white wine
1 teaspoon green peppercorns, lightly crushed
6 tablespoons unsalted butter, in pieces
2 teaspoons chopped fresh mint
Salt, to taste

1. Cut beans in half lengthwise. Peel carrots, then slice carrots and zucchini into ribbons, using a mandolin or vegetable peeler; set aside.

Rinse scallops, remove any dark strands; pat dry with paper towels.
2. Put lemon juice, wine and peppercorns into a saucepan and bring to a boil. Simmer 3 to 4 minutes, then add scallops, cover and cook gently 3 to 5 minutes, until scallops are firm and opaque. Remove with a slotted spoon and keep warm.

3. Boil the pan juices until reduced to about 1 tablespoon. Over a very low heat, beat in butter a small piece at a time, to form a smooth shiny sauce. Stir in mint and salt and keep warm.

Blanch beans, carrots and zucchini in boiling water 1 minute; drain and arrange in a "nest" shape on 4 warmed plates. Pile scallops in the center and pour sauce over the top. Serve immediately.

Makes 4 servings.

Scallops in Tomato Cream

3 ripe tomatoes
1 pound shelled sea scallops
1 tablespoon sunflower oil
1 small leek, white part only, finely chopped
1/4 cup dry vermouth
1/4 cup dry white wine
2/3 cup fromage frais or crème fraîche
8 basil leaves, torn
Salt and pepper, to taste
TO GARNISH:
Basil sprigs

1. Plunge tomatoes into a bowl of boiling water 1 minute, then peel away skins. Cut in half and squeeze out seeds; finely chop tomato flesh.

Rinse scallops, remove any dark strands; pat dry with paper towels.
2. In a frying pan, heat oil, add leek and fry gently about 5 minutes, until softened. Add vermouth and wine and bring to a boil, reduce heat, then simmer 2 minutes. Add scallops, cover and cook 3 to 5 minutes, until opaque and firm. Remove with a slot-ted spoon and keep warm.
3. Boil liquid remaining in pan until reduced to 2 tablespoons. Add tomatoes and heat through. Stir in fromage frais and torn basil and heat through; do not boil. Season with salt and pepper.

Spoon the sauce onto 4 warmed plates, pile scallops in the center and garnish with basil sprigs. Serve as a starter or light lunch.

Makes 4 servings.

Spicy Stir-Fried Abalone

2 abalone in shells or 12 ounces abalone meat
2 tablespoons sunflower oil
1 garlic clove, chopped
1 teaspoon chopped gingerroot
1 dried red chile
2 tablespoons soy sauce
2 tablespoons rice wine or dry sherry
1 teaspoon sugar
1 teaspoon tomato paste
1 tablespoon shredded green onion

1. First shell abalone. Push the tip of an oyster knife (or other strong small knife) into the thin end of the shell underneath the flesh. Work the blade until the muscle is free. Take out the white meat; rinse thoroughly, discarding the intestine. Pat dry with paper towels.
2. Cut abalone into very thin slices, then pound with a mallet until limp and velvety to tenderize.
3. In a wok or frying pan, heat oil and briefly fry garlic, gingerroot and chile. Add abalone and stir-fry 30 seconds. Remove abalone with a slotted spoon.

Add soy sauce, rice wine, sugar and tomato paste to pan. Bring to a boil, then simmer 2 minutes. Return abalone to pan and heat through.

Remove chile and sprinkle with shredded green onion to serve. Serve as a light lunch.

Makes 4 servings.

Spicy Shrimp & Chinese Pancakes

2-1/2 cups all-purpose flour
A little sesame oil
1 pound raw large shrimp in shells
1 tablespoon peanut oil
1 teaspoon finely chopped gingerroot
2 teaspoons finely chopped green onion
1 tablespoon rice wine or dry sherry
2 teaspoons soy sauce
1/2 teaspoon chili bean sauce
1 teaspoon tomato paste
2 teaspoons *each* honey and lemon juice
TO SERVE:
Hoisin sauce
1/2 cucumber, julienned
4 green onions, julienned

1. Sift flour into a bowl. Gradually add 1-1/8 cups very hot water, mixing with a fork or chopsticks to a soft dough. Knead on a lightly floured surface 5 minutes. Put in a plastic bag and leave 30 minutes. Knead briefly, then form in a roll, 18 inches long; cut in 16 pieces.

2. Shape 2 pieces of dough in balls. Dip 1 ball in sesame oil and place on top of the other. Roll out the 2 balls together to a 6-inch round. Repeat with remaining dough. Heat a wok or large nonstick frying pan (without added oil) and cook pancakes until lightly browned, turning once. When cool enough to handle, peel pancakes apart, wrap in foil and keep warm in a steamer.

3. Peel shrimp, leaving tail intact, slit down the back and remove dark vein. Heat oil in wok or frying pan, add gingerroot and green onion and stir-fry briefly. Add shrimp and stir-fry 1 to 2 minutes, until pink. Add remaining ingredients and simmer 3 minutes. Turn into a warmed serving dish.

To eat, each person spreads pancakes with a little hoisin sauce, adds a shrimp and a little cucumber and green onion, then rolls. Serve as a starter.

Makes 4 servings.

Shrimp Satay

1-1/2 pounds large raw shrimp in shells
1 teaspoon ground turmeric
1 teaspoon ground cumin
1/2 teaspoon ground fennel
1/2 teaspoon finely minced lemon peel
1 tablespoon light brown sugar
1/4 cup cream of coconut
DIP:
1 red chile
2 tablespoons honey
1/4 cup cider vinegar
6 thin cucumber slices
TO GARNISH:
Parsley sprigs

1. To peel shrimp, pull off tail and shell.

2. Using a small sharp knife, slit down center back and remove dark vein. Soak bamboo skewers in water.

In a bowl, mix together spices, lemon peel, sugar and cream of coconut. Add shrimp, cover and refrigerate 1 to 2 hours, stirring occasionally.

To prepare dip, wearing rubber gloves, cut chile in half lengthwise, carefully remove and discard seeds. Finely chop chile and mix with honey and vinegar. Cut cucumber slices in quarters and add to dip. Divide among 4 tiny serving dishes. Preheat broiler.

3. Thread shrimp onto bamboo skewers and cook under preheated broiler 5 to 6 minutes, turning occasionally. Arrange on 4 plates and garnish with parsley. Serve immediately, with the dip, as a starter.

Makes 4 servings.

Singapore Lettuce Cups

1 red chile
3 ounces small green beans
3 ounces bean sprouts
1/4 cucumber, chopped
8 ounces peeled, cooked shrimp, thawed if frozen
3 tablespoons shredded green onion
1 tablespoon chopped cilantro
1 lettuce head
Cilantro leaves, to garnish
DRESSING:
1/3 cup shelled peanuts, roasted
1 teaspoon soy sauce
1 garlic clove, crushed
1 teaspoon light brown sugar
1/4 cup orange juice
1 tablespoon lemon juice

1. Wear rubber gloves to prepare chile: cut in half, carefully discard stem and seeds; then chop finely. Cut beans in short lengths and blanch in boiling water 2 minutes. Blanch bean sprouts for a few seconds. Drain vegetables and refresh under cold running water. Mix together chile, beans, bean sprouts, cucumber, shrimp, green onion and cilantro.
2. To make dressing, in a food processor, coarsely grind peanuts, then mix with soy sauce, garlic, sugar, orange and lemon juices. Taste and add salt if necessary. Add to shrimp mixture and stir well.
3. Separate lettuce leaves. Place a spoonful of shrimp mixture on each leaf. Arrange on a serving platter and garnish with cilantro leaves. Serve as a starter.

Makes 6 to 8 servings.

Shrimp & Coconut Fritters

8 ounces peeled shrimp, thawed if frozen
4 green onions, chopped
2 tablespoons cream of coconut
3 ounces bean sprouts, roughly chopped
3/4 cup all-purpose flour
1 teaspoon baking powder
2 garlic cloves, crushed
1 teaspoon chopped gingerroot
2 eggs, beaten
1 teaspoon salt and pepper, to taste
1 teaspoon soy sauce
Vegetable oil for deep-frying
TO GARNISH:
Lettuce leaves
Lime slices
Shredded green onion

1. Put shrimp and green onions into a blender or food processor; process until finely chopped. Add remaining ingredients except oil and garnish to blender or food processor. Process a few seconds to mix.

2. Heat oil to 350F (175C) or until a little mixture dropped into oil immediately rises to surface. Drop spoons of mixture, a few at a time, into oil and cook 3 to 4 minutes, until puffy and golden-brown. Remove with a slotted spoon and drain on paper towels. Keep warm while cooking remaining mixture.

3. Arrange lettuce leaves on individual plates. Make a cut through to the center of each lime slice, then twist. Pile fritters onto lettuce leaves and garnish with shredded green onion and lime twists. Serve hot, as a starter.

Makes 4 to 6 servings.

Shrimp & Leek Timbales

4 leeks
8 ounces peeled shrimp, thawed if frozen
1 teaspoon chopped dill
Pinch of grated nutmeg
2 egg whites
2 tablespoons whipping cream
Salt and pepper, to taste
1/2 cup fish stock and white wine mixed
1 shallot, finely chopped
4 ounces unsalted butter, in small pieces
1 teaspoon coarsely ground peppercorns
TO GARNISH:
4 whole cooked shrimp in shells
4 dill sprigs

1. Preheat oven to 375F (190C). Cut leeks in half lengthwise. Blanch in boiling salted water 1 to 2 minutes until slightly softened, then refresh under cold running water.

Line the bottom and sides of 4 small buttered molds or ramekins with the leeks, arranging the pieces like the spokes of a wheel and allowing them to overhang the edge of the dishes.

2. Place shrimp, chopped dill, nutmeg, egg whites, cream, salt and pepper in a blender or food processor and process until smooth. Fill prepared molds with the mixture; fold leek strips over to enclose, trimming if necessary. Place in a baking pan half filled with hot water and bake 15 to 20 minutes, until firm.

3. Place stock mixture and shallot in a small pan, bring to a boil and boil rapidly until reduced to about 2 tablespoons. Reduce heat to very low and whisk in butter, piece by piece, until smooth and glossy.

Turn the timbales out onto 4 warmed plates and pour the sauce around them. Sprinkle with pepper and garnish with shrimp and dill sprigs. Serve as a starter.

Makes 4 servings.

Shrimp & Salmon Rolls

1 egg yolk
1/2 teaspoon Dijon-style mustard
Salt and pepper, to taste
2/3 cup olive oil and sunflower oil mixed
1 tablespoon lemon juice
1 ounce watercress, chopped
1 celery stalk, finely chopped
8 ounces peeled cooked shrimp, thawed if frozen
12 slices smoked salmon
TO GARNISH:
Chicory
Orange slices

1. In a bowl, blend egg yolk, mustard, salt and pepper; add oil drop by drop, beating thoroughly between each addition. As mayonnaise thickens, increase the flow of oil to a slow steady stream, beating constantly. Beat in lemon juice and check seasoning.
2. Stir in watercress, celery and shrimp. Lay smoked salmon slices on a work surface. Spoon equal amounts of filling onto each slice.
3. Roll up salmon carefully, enclosing the shrimp filling. Arrange 2 salmon rolls on each place and garnish with chicory and orange slices. Serve with brown bread and butter, as a starter or light lunch.

Makes 6 servings.

Shrimp in Noodle Baskets

3 ounces bean thread (cellophane) noodles
Sunflower oil for frying
1 (1-inch) cucumber slice
1/4 cup unsalted butter
1 garlic clove, crushed
8 ounces peeled shrimp, thawed if frozen
2 tablespoons lemon juice
2 tablespoons snipped chives
Salt and pepper, to taste
2 tablespoons brandy

1. Cut noodles in 4 equal heaps using scissors or a sharp knife. In a small saucepan, heat about 1 inch of oil. Carefully add 1 heap of noodles—it will immediately expand to fit the saucepan. Quickly turn noodles over, cook a few seconds, then drain well on paper towels. Keep warm while cooking remaining noodles.
2. Cut cucumber in matchstick pieces. In a frying pan, heat butter, add garlic and fry 1 minute. Add shrimp and stir-fry quickly until pink. Add cucumber, lemon juice, chives, salt and pepper and cook 1 minute.
3. Warm brandy and pour quickly over shrimp. Ignite and leave until flames have gone out. Place noodle baskets on 4 warmed plates. Spoon shrimp mixture into center and serve immediately, as a starter.

Makes 4 servings.

Buttery Shrimp Boxes

1 large unsliced day-old sandwich loaf
6 tablespoons unsalted butter
1 shallot, finely chopped
4 ounces peeled small shrimp
2 ounces small button mushrooms
3 tablespoons dry white wine
2 ounces soft cheese with garlic and herbs
1/4 cup half and half
Salt and pepper, to taste
TO GARNISH:
Chicory
Dill sprigs

1. Preheat oven to 375F (190C). Remove crusts from loaf and cut bread crosswise into 4 equal slices. Mark out a square 1/2 inch from the edges of each slice, then cut down to within 1/2 inch of the other side of the slice. Pull out the crumbs carefully, forming a container.

2. Melt 4 tablespoons butter and brush liberally over the boxes, inside and out. Put on a baking sheet and bake 20 to 25 minutes, until crisp and golden-brown.

3. Meanwhile, prepare filling. In a small frying pan, melt remaining butter, add shallot and fry about 5 min-utes, until softened. Add shrimp and mushrooms and cook quickly until shrimp are pink and mushrooms are slightly softened. Stir in wine, bring to a boil and cook until reduced by half. Reduce heat and stir in cheese until melted. Add half and half, salt and pepper and stir well until thick and creamy.

Put the boxes on 4 plates garnished with chicory. Fill with shrimp mixture and garnish with dill. Serve warm, as a starter.

Makes 4 servings.

Shrimp & Spinach Soufflé

1 pound spinach leaves
Grated nutmeg, salt and pepper, to taste
3 tablespoons butter
1/4 cup all-purpose flour
2/3 cup milk
1 tablespoon lemon juice
1/2 cup shredded Cheddar cheese
6 ounces peeled small shrimp
3 eggs, separated
4 teaspoons sesame seeds

1. Preheat oven to 375F (190C). Put spinach into a large saucepan with just the water clinging to leaves after washing; season with nutmeg, salt and pepper. Bring to a boil, then cover and cook 5 minutes, until softened. Drain in a sieve, pressing out as much water as possible. Turn onto a board and chop finely. Drain again, then set aside.

2. In a saucepan, melt butter, add flour and cook 1 minute. Gradually stir in milk, cooking until thickened and smooth.

Remove from heat and stir in lemon juice, cheese, shrimp, spinach, egg yolks, salt and pepper; stir well. In a bowl, whisk egg whites until stiff, then fold carefully into mixture.

3. Butter a 5-cup soufflé dish and sprinkle with half the sesame seeds. Spoon mixture into dish and sprinkle with remaining sesame seeds. Put on a baking sheet and bake 35 minutes, until puffed and golden-brown. Serve immediately, with a salad, as a starter or light lunch.

Makes 4 servings.

Shrimp Fettuccine

1 ounce prosciutto
12 basil leaves
6 tablespoons unsalted butter
2 garlic cloves, crushed
4 ounces peeled shrimp
12 ounces fresh spinach fettuccine
1/4 cup grated Parmesan cheese
Salt and pepper, to taste

1. Cut prosciutto in julienne strips. Tear basil leaves in half. In a large skillet, melt butter, add garlic and fry gently 1 minute. Add prosciutto, shrimp and basil and cook 2 minutes. Keep warm while cooking pasta.
2. Bring a large saucepan of salted water to a boil, add fettuccine and cook 3 minutes, or until *al dente;* drain thoroughly.
3. Add half the Parmesan cheese and salt and pepper to the sauce, stir well.

Add the fettuccine and toss thoroughly to coat with the sauce.

Divide among 4 plates and sprinkle with remaining Parmesan cheese. Serve piping hot, with a green side salad.

Makes 4 servings.

Note: Substitute 8 ounces dried fettuccine for fresh and cook 10 to 12 minutes.

Shrimp Risotto

1 pound cooked shrimp in shells
1 bay leaf
Few celery leaves
6 peppercorns
Salt, to taste
Few saffron threads
6 tablespoons butter
1 onion, chopped
1 garlic clove, crushed
2 cups Italian Arborio rice
1-1/4 cups dry white wine
2 zucchini, cut into strips
6 ounces oyster mushrooms, cut into pieces
2 tablespoons chopped parsley
4 tablespoons grated Parmesan cheese

1. Peel shrimp; set aside. Wash shells, then put in a saucepan with bay leaf, celery leaves, peppercorns, salt, saffron and 3-3/4 cups water. Bring to a boil, then simmer 20 minutes. Strain and reserve stock.

2. In a heavy saucepan, melt half the butter, add onion and garlic and cook about 5 minutes, until softened but not colored. Add rice and stir to coat all the grains with butter. Add one-third of the reserved stock and bring to a boil, then simmer, uncovered, until stock is absorbed. Gradually add more stock and wine until it has all been absorbed and the rice is cooked; this will take about 20 minutes.

3. In a separate pan, melt remaining butter, add shrimp, zucchini and mushrooms and cook 2 to 3 minutes. Fold into rice, with parsley and half the Parmesan cheese; taste and add salt, if needed.

Serve piping hot, sprinkled with remaining Parmesan cheese.

Makes 4 servings.

Langostinos & Rice

16 to 24 cooked small langostinos
1-1/4 cups long-grain rice
1/4 cup wild rice
1/4 cup butter, softened
2 teaspoons chopped fresh tarragon
2 teaspoons snipped chives
1 garlic clove, crushed
2 tablespoons sunflower oil
1 zucchini, cut in thin strips
1 carrot, cut in thin strips
1/2 teaspoon cumin seeds
4 ounces oyster mushrooms, cut in pieces
1/2 cup fish stock
Salt and pepper, to taste

1. Rinse langostinos, then remove shells: twist off the head, then gently pull off the tail shell and remove the body shell. Cut down the back and remove dark vein. Dry well with paper towels; set aside.
2. Cook both rices in 3 cups of boiling salted water 10 to 12 minutes, until tender and water is absorbed.

In a small bowl, blend butter, tarragon, chives and garlic together; set aside.
3. In a frying pan, heat half the oil, add langostinos and stir-fry quickly, until pink. Remove from pan and keep warm. Heat remaining oil in pan, add zucchini and carrot and stir-fry 1 to 2 minutes. Add cumin seeds and mushrooms and stir well.

Add rice, langostinos, stock and salt and pepper, bring to a boil, cover and cook gently 2 to 3 minutes.

Just before serving, stir in the herb butter; alternatively, serve mixture on individual plates, topped with a lump of herb butter.

Makes 4 servings.

Note: Langostinos are also called Dublin Bay prawns in Britain and scampi in Italy.

Seafood Kabobs & Mango Sauce

1-1/2 pounds cooked small langostinos
1 tablespoon olive oil
1 tablespoon lemon juice
1 tablespoon chopped fennel
1 tablespoon chopped parsley
Salt and pepper, to taste
1 ripe mango
8 bacon slices
8 green onions
1 tablespoon honey
Dash Tabasco sauce
1 garlic clove, crushed
1/4 cup orange juice
1 teaspoon soy sauce

1. Peel langostinos, leaving tail section intact: twist off the head and carefully remove the body shell. Cut down the center back and remove dark vein. Soak bamboo skewers.

In a bowl, mix together oil, lemon juice, fennel, parsley, salt and pepper. Add langostinos and stir well. Cover and refrigerate while preparing remaining ingredients.

2. Peel mango and cut in half, along one side of seed; remove seed. Cut one half in 16 cubes. Cut each bacon slice in half and wrap around a mango cube. Halve green onions. Preheat broiler.

3. Thread marinated langostinos, bacon-wrapped mango and green onions onto 8 skewers.

Roughly chop remaining mango and put into a blender or food processor with honey, Tabasco sauce, garlic, orange juice and soy sauce. Blend until smooth; transfer to a saucepan and heat through gently.

Put the seafood kabobs under preheated broiler and cook 6 to 8 minutes, turning occasionally, until bacon is crisp. Serve hot with mango sauce.

Makes 4 servings.

Note: Langostinos are the same species as Dublin Bay prawns and scampi.

Langostinos & Pear Salad

24 to 32 cooked langostinos
1 beefsteak tomato, peeled and seeded
1 teaspoon chopped fresh basil
3 tablespoons plain yogurt
Salt and pepper, to taste
2 small pears
2 teaspoons lemon juice
Mache or lamb's lettuce
Radicchio
Chicory
Lettuce leaves
TO GARNISH:
Chervil sprigs

1. Remove shells: twist off the head, gently pull off the tail shell and remove body shell. Cut down the back and remove dark vein.

2. Finely chop tomato; set half aside for garnish. Put the other half in a blender or food processor with the basil, yogurt, salt and pepper; blend until smooth.

Peel, core and thinly slice pears.

Place half a sliced pear on each serving plate and brush with lemon juice. Arrange the langostinos alongside. Place a few salad leaves on each plate.

3. Pour a little tomato cream over the shellfish and top with a little chopped tomato. Garnish with chervil and serve as a starter or light lunch.

Makes 4 servings.

Grilled Lobster

2 (1-1/2-lb.) live lobsters
2 teaspoons green peppercorns
1/2 cup unsalted butter
2 tablespoons finely chopped parsley
1 tablespoon chopped fresh mixed herbs (basil, tarragon, dill, mint)
2 teaspoons lemon juice
Salt and pepper, to taste
TO GARNISH:
Lettuce leaves

1. Secure lobster claws with rubber bands. To prepare each lobster, hold underside down on a board. Place the point of a strong knife at the point where the body and tail join and plunge it quickly down through the lobster. It will be killed instantly. Cut along the body and tail firmly to split the lobster in half.
2. Remove the stomach sac near the eyes, and black intestinal thread which runs the length of the body. Take out the grey-green liver, and coral if any; these can be used in sauces. Carefully rinse and pat dry lobsters with paper towels.
　Crush peppercorns coarsely and mix with butter, herbs, lemon juice and salt and pepper. Dot half the butter over lobster flesh. Shape the rest in a roll, wrap in foil and chill.
3. Preheat broiler. Slit underside of lobsters in several places. Cook lobster halves under broiler 12 to 15 minutes, until flesh is opaque. Slice butter roll and arrange on lobster flesh. Serve on a bed of lettuce leaves, as a starter or light lunch.

Makes 4 servings.

Note: This sophisticated dish may alternatively be served as a main course for two.

Lobster Salad

4 (1-lb.) live lobsters
Salt and pepper, to taste
DRESSING:
1 tablespoon sesame oil
2 tablespoons olive oil
1/2 teaspoon Dijon-style mustard
2 teaspoons white wine vinegar
Salt and pepper, to taste
2 tablespoons toasted sesame seeds
TO SERVE:
2 carrots
1 small celery root
Snipped chives

1. Secure lobster claws with rubber bands. Put lobsters, head down, in a large pan of fast boiling salted water. Cover, bring to a boil and simmer 12 minutes until shells are bright red. Remove from pan; cool under running water until lobsters are cool enough to handle.

Snap off legs and break each apart at the central joint; remove flesh with a skewer. Snap each claw free near the body, then crack the claw shells with a mallet and remove flesh in one piece if possible.

2. With the lobster on its back, cut down either side of the shell, then pull away the bony covering which protects the underside. Pry the flesh free in one piece, starting at the tail. Discard the stomach sac near the eyes and the dark intestinal thread which runs the length of the body. Take out the grey-green liver, and coral if any; these can be used in sauces.

3. Rinse and dry lobster shells and place on 4 individual serving plates. Slice tail meat in medallions and arrange in the shells with remaining meat. Mix together dressing ingredients and pour over lobster. Shred carrots and celery root; place a little on each plate and sprinkle with chives. Serve as a starter or a light meal.

Makes 4 servings.

Lobster Filo Bundles

1/4 cup butter
2 tablespoons chopped watercress
Salt and pepper, to taste
6 ounces cooked lobster meat
8 sheets filo pastry
Melted butter for brushing
TOMATO SAUCE:
1 pound tomatoes, peeled, seeded and chopped
1 teaspoon tomato paste
Pinch of sugar
8 to 10 basil leaves, chopped
TO GARNISH:
Snipped chives and lemon twists

1. Preheat oven to 400F (205C). Make sauce as in step 3. In a bowl, blend together butter, watercress and salt and pepper. Roughly chop lobster meat. Brush one sheet of filo pastry with melted butter; fold in half and brush again with butter. Put a little lobster meat near one short edge and spread with watercress butter.
2. Roll up pastry to enclose lobster, tucking in the ends to form a bundle. Repeat with remaining filo pastry, lobster and watercress butter. Place the bundles on a greased baking sheet and brush again with melted butter.

Bake 15 minutes, until golden-brown.
3. To make sauce, put tomatoes in a saucepan with tomato paste, sugar and salt and pepper; simmer gently about 15 to 20 minutes, until thickened. Stir basil leaves into sauce.

Arrange 2 lobster bundles and a little tomato sauce on each serving plate and sprinkle chives over sauce. Garnish with lemon twists and serve as a light meal.

Makes 4 servings.

Lobster & Spinach Roulade

1 pound fresh spinach
Pinch of grated nutmeg
1/4 cup grated Parmesan cheese
4 eggs, separated
Salt and pepper, to taste
FILLING:
2 tablespoons butter
1/4 cup all-purpose flour
1 cup milk
2 tomatoes, peeled and seeded
6 ounces cooked lobster meat
2 teaspoons chopped dill
2 tablespoons lime juice

1. Preheat oven to 375F (190C). Grease and line an 11 x 7-inch jelly-roll pan.

Put spinach into a saucepan with just the water clinging to the leaves after washing. Cover and cook 5 minutes, until softened. Drain well, pressing out as much water as possible. Chop finely, then place in a bowl with nutmeg, Parmesan cheese, egg yolks and salt and pepper; mix well.

In a bowl, whisk egg whites until stiff, then fold into spinach mixture. Pour into prepared pan; spread to level mixture. Bake 15 minutes, until firm.

2. Meanwhile, make filling. In a saucepan, melt butter, add flour and cook 1 minute. Gradually add milk, stirring until thickened and smooth. Simmer 2 minutes. Chop tomatoes and lobster; stir into sauce with dill, lime juice and salt and pepper to taste; heat through.

3. Invert the roulade onto a sheet of waxed paper and carefully remove lining paper. Cover with filling and roll up from a short edge, using the waxed paper to lift the roulade.

Cut in slices and serve warm, as a light meal or starter.

Makes 4 to 6 servings.

Lobster with Hollandaise

2 carrots, sliced
2 onions, sliced
Bouquet garni
1-3/4 cups white wine
Few fennel stalks
Few black peppercorns
2 (1-1/2-lb.) live lobsters
HOLLANDAISE SAUCE:
2 eggs
2 tablespoons lemon juice
Salt, to taste
2 teaspoons pink peppercorns, crushed
3/4 cup unsalted butter

1. In a large saucepan, put carrots, onions, bouquet garni, wine, fennel, peppercorns and 2 cups cold water. Bring to a boil, then simmer 5 minutes. Bring to a fast boil, add lobsters, cover and bring back to a boil. Cook 18 minutes, or until shells are bright red. Cool under running water.

2. Meanwhile, make sauce. Put eggs, lemon juice, salt and peppercorns into a blender or food processor and blend for a few seconds. Heat butter until foaming; pour half into blender or food processor and blend for a few seconds. Pour in remaining butter and blend 5 to 7 seconds, until thick and creamy. Pour into a heatproof bowl set over a saucepan of hot water and leave until thickened, stirring occasionally.

3. To prepare each lobster, first kill as on page 88. Lay it on its back and, using a heavy sharp knife, cut through firmly from head to tail to split lobster in half; separate lobster halves. Discard the stomach sac near the eyes and the dark intestinal thread running the length of the body. Take out the liver and any coral.

Arrange the lobster halves on 4 plates and spoon the sauce over the meat. Serve, as a light meal, with salad.

Makes 4 servings.

Lobster Tails in Sorrel Sauce

8 lobster tails
2 cups fish stock
1/2 cup dry white wine
1/4 cup dry vermouth
1 cup whipping cream
1 tablespoon lemon juice
Salt and pepper, to taste
4 tablespoons butter, softened
8 ounces young sorrel leaves, shredded
TO GARNISH:
Orange slices

1. Place lobster tails top-side down on a board and, using a strong sharp knife, cut through the lobster tails, splitting them in half. Discard the dark intestinal vein and remove the meat from the shells in one piece. Rinse well and dry on paper towels.
2. In a saucepan, boil stock, wine and vermouth until reduced to 1 cup. Add cream and simmer until reduced again to 1 cup. Add lobster tails and cook gently 5 minutes; remove with a slotted spoon and keep warm.
3. Add lemon juice, salt and pepper to the sauce. Beat in butter, a little at a time. Add sorrel and cook until just wilted.

Arrange lobster tails on 4 warmed dishes and pour over the sauce.

Garnish with orange slices and serve as a light meal.

Makes 4 servings.

Strawberry-dressed Crayfish

1 cup dry white wine
1 small onion, chopped
1 carrot, chopped
1 leek, chopped
1 celery stalk, chopped
Bouquet garni
Salt and pepper, to taste
2 pounds live crayfish
STRAWBERRY DRESSING:
4 ounces strawberries
2 tablespoons vegetable oil
3 tablespoons lemon juice
1 teaspoon coarse-grain mustard
TO SERVE:
Lettuce leaves (red lettuce, chicory)

1. Put wine, onion, carrot, leek, celery, bouquet garni, salt and pepper and 2 cups cold water into a large saucepan, bring to a boil and simmer 5 minutes. Add crayfish, cover and cook 5 minutes or until they turn red. Drain and rinse with cold water to cool.
2. Reserve 4 crayfish in shells for garnish. Peel the rest, by carefully twisting off the heads and peeling away the tail shells.

Arrange lettuce leaves on 4 plates and arrange crayfish on top. Set the reserved crayfish to one side of the plate.
3. To make dressing, press strawberries through a sieve into a bowl. Add oil, lemon juice, mustard, salt and pepper; mix well. Drizzle over the salad to serve.

Makes 4 servings.

Crayfish Salad

20 live crayfish
1 pink grapefruit
4 ounces small green beans, halved
8 ounces thin asparagus spears
1 beefsteak tomato
1 avocado
8 oyster mushrooms
4 large lettuce leaves
1 orange
1/2 cup unsalted butter
1 teaspoon Dijon-style mustard
Salt and pepper, to taste

1. Put crayfish into a large saucepan of boiling water. Bring to a boil, then simmer about 5 minutes, until they turn red. Drain and rinse with cold water to cool. Set aside 4 crayfish for garnish. Peel the rest, twisting off the heads and peeling away the tail shells; set aside.

2. Remove peel and white pith from grapefruit; cut between membrane into sections, over a bowl.

Blanch beans and asparagus in boiling water 4 minutes, then cool quickly under cold running water. Peel, seed and finely chop tomato. Peel, quarter and thinly slice avocado. Blanch mushrooms.

3. Place lettuce on 4 plates. Arrange vegetables on plates, alternating colors and placing a few grapefruit sections in center.

Squeeze the juice from the orange and put in a small saucepan with butter, mustard, salt and pepper. Heat gently until butter has melted, whisking constantly. Add crayfish and heat through briefly. Remove crayfish with a slotted spoon and arrange on the lettuce. Pour over the sauce, garnish with reserved whole crayfish and serve immediately.

Makes 4 servings.

Crab & Orange Salad

2 (1-1/2 lb.) crab, freshly boiled (see page 44)
1 Belgium endive
2 oranges
3 ounces alfalfa sprouts
Few leaves chicory
ORANGE DRESSING:
2 tablespoons orange juice
2 teaspoons Japanese soy sauce
2 tablespoons sunflower oil
1 tablespoon lemon juice
1 tablespoon walnut oil
Salt and pepper, to taste
TO GARNISH:
Shredded green onion tops

1. Place crab shell-down on a work surface. Twist off claws and legs. Crack shell of each claw and extract meat. Break apart the legs and remove meat with a skewer. Twist free the apron on underside of crab and discard.
2. Insert a strong knife between main shell and underside and pry upwards to detach the underside. Scoop out and reserve meat from main shell, discarding the small greyish-white stomach sac and its appendages, just behind the crab's mouth.
3. Pull away the soft grey feather gills along the edges of the underside and discard. Using a heavy knife, split the underside down the middle; remove flesh from the crevices using a skewer.

Separate endive leaves; peel and section oranges, discarding all white pith. Arrange endive and orange sections alternately in fan shapes on 4 plates. Place the alfalfa and chicory at the base; pile crab meat on top.

Put dressing ingredients into a jar with a lid, shake well and pour over the salad. Sprinkle crab with green onion and serve as a starter.

Makes 4 servings.

Potted Crab & Vegetables

2 pounds crab, freshly boiled (see page 44)
1/2 cup unsalted butter
1/4 teaspoon ground mace
1/4 teaspoon ground allspice
2 pinches red (cayenne) pepper
Freshly ground black pepper
4 tablespoons clarified butter (see below)
4 tarragon sprigs
8 ears of baby corn
8 asparagus tips
2 ounces snow peas
Oak leaf lettuce
Chicory
2 tablespoons lemon vinaigrette

1. Remove crab meat from shell (see opposite page). Put white and brown meat in a bowl and mix with a fork. In a saucepan, melt butter, add crab, mace, allspice, cayenne and black pepper; mix well.
2. Spoon mixture into 4 ramekin dishes, pressing down lightly. Heat clarified butter and pour gently over the top. Garnish with tarragon. Cool, then cover and refrigerate about 2 hours, until firm.
3. Blanch corn, asparagus and snow peas in boiling salted water 1 minute. Cool quickly under cold running water; drain well. Place ramekin dish-
es on 4 large plates and surround with lettuce, chicory and vegetables. Just before serving, drizzle a little vinaigrette over each salad. Serve with whole-wheat toast as a starter or light lunch.

Makes 4 servings.

Clarified Butter: Melt 1/2 cup salted butter in a pan, then heat until foaming stops, without browning. Let stand until white particles have sunk to the bottom, leaving clear yellow liquid. Strain liquid carefully through muslin into a bowl.

Crab Mousse with Cucumber

8 ounces crabmeat (white and brown)
1 tablespoon lemon juice
1/4 teaspoon finely grated lemon peel
5 teaspoons unflavored gelatin powder
1/4 cup fish stock or water
4 (3-oz.) packages cream cheese, softened
1 tablespoon dry sherry
Salt and pepper, to taste
2 egg whites
1 cucumber
1 tablespoon chopped dill
1 tablespoon white wine vinegar
1 teaspoon Dijon-style mustard
2 tablespoons vegetable oil
TO GARNISH:
Dill sprigs and red lumpfish roe

1. In a bowl, mix together brown and white crabmeat, with lemon juice and peel. Sprinkle gelatin over stock in a small saucepan. Let stand until softened. Heat until dissolved.

2. Put crab, dissolved gelatin, cream cheese, sherry and pepper into a blender or food processor and blend until smooth. Taste and add salt if necessary. Turn into a bowl. Whisk egg whites until stiff, then fold into crab mixture.

Turn mixture into a dampened 3-3/4-cup mold and smooth the top. Cover and refrigerate mousse about 4 hours, until set.·

3. Cut grooves along the cucumber skin with a zester, then slice thinly. In a small bowl, whisk dill, vinegar, mustard, oil, salt and pepper together until smooth.

Turn crab mousse out onto a serving plate and arrange overlapping slices of cucumber around the edge. Drizzle the dressing over the cucumber and garnish with dill sprigs and lumpfish roe. Serve as a starter or light meal.

Makes 4 to 6 servings.

Deviled Crab

4 (1-lb.) crab, freshly boiled (see page 44)
1 small onion
2 ounces button mushrooms
1 celery stalk
4 tablespoons butter
1 teaspoon prepared horseradish
2 teaspoons Dijon-style mustard
1 tablespoon Worcestershire sauce
2 tablespoons all-purpose flour
2 tablespoons dry white wine
2 tablespoons whipping cream
Salt and pepper, to taste
1/2 cup bread crumbs, toasted
1 tablespoon grated Parmesan cheese
TO GARNISH:
Snipped chives

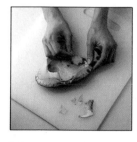  

1. Remove crabmeat from shells (as described on page 96). When all the meat has been removed, break away the shell edge along the natural dark rim of the shell. Scrub shells.

2. Finely chop onion, mushrooms and celery. In a frying pan, melt half the butter, add the vegetables and fry gently about 5 minutes, until softened. Add horseradish, mustard and Worcestershire sauce and stir well.

Stir in the flour and cook 1 minute, stirring. Stir in wine and cream and cook, stirring, until thickened and smooth. Remove from heat and fold in crabmeat; season with salt and pepper.

3. Preheat broiler. Spoon mixture into crab shells and sprinkle with bread crumbs and cheese. Place under preheated broiler 3 to 4 minutes, until golden-brown.

Serve warm, topped with chives and accompanied by a salad.

Makes 4 servings.

Crab Ravioli with Baby Corn

RAVIOLI DOUGH:
2 cups bread flour
1/2 teaspoon salt
2 eggs, beaten
1 tablespoon olive oil
FILLING:
10 ounces crabmeat (white and brown)
2 tablespoons butter
Few drops of chili sauce
SAUCE:
6 tablespoons butter
6 ounces baby corn
2 tablespoons lemon juice
12 small basil leaves
TO SERVE:
Grated Parmesan cheese

1. To make dough, sift flour and salt onto a work surface; make a well in the center and add eggs and oil. Gradually mix in flour to form a soft dough; knead 10 minutes. Wrap in foil and leave 1 hour.

2. Meanwhile, prepare filling. Flake crabmeat into a bowl. Melt butter and add to crab with chili sauce and salt and pepper to taste.

On a floured surface, roll out half the dough to a 16-inch square. Using a knife, mark the dough in 2-inch squares; do not cut. Put a little crab mixture into the center of each square. Brush along the edges of each square with water.

Roll out remaining dough to the same size and place over the filling. Press down between the filling to seal the squares, then cut in pockets. Cook in a large saucepan of boiling salted water 3 to 4 minutes; drain and keep warm.

3. To make sauce, in a saucepan, melt butter, add corn and cook, stirring, 2 to 3 minutes. Stir in lemon juice, basil, salt and pepper.

Arrange the ravioli on 4 warmed plates and pour the sauce over the top. Sprinkle with Parmesan cheese and serve immediately.

Makes 4 servings.

Crab Burritos

1 tablespoon vegetable oil
1 small onion, finely chopped
1 pound tomatoes, peeled and chopped
1 tablespoon tomato paste
1/4 teaspoon red (cayenne) pepper
1 teaspoon paprika
2 teaspoons Worcestershire sauce
Salt and pepper, to taste
8 tortillas or crepes
6 ounces white crabmeat
2 ounces mozzarella cheese, shredded (1/2 cup)
Shredded lettuce
1 avocado
1 tablespoon lemon juice
4 tablespoons dairy sour cream

1. Preheat oven to 350F (175C). Grease an ovenproof dish.

In a saucepan, heat oil, add onion and fry until softened. Add tomatoes, tomato paste, cayenne, paprika, Worcestershire sauce, salt and pepper. Bring to a boil, then simmer, uncovered, about 20 minutes, until thick.

2. Spread a little sauce over each tortilla, sprinkle with crabmeat and mozzarella, then roll up, tucking in the ends. Put into prepared dish, cover and bake 20 minutes.

3. Place lettuce on individual serving plates. Peel and slice avocado, brush with lemon juice and arrange on the lettuce. Place 2 burritos on each plate and top with the tomato sauce and a spoonful of sour cream. Serve any remaining tomato sauce separately.

Makes 4 servings.

Squid & Red Pepper Salad

1-1/2 pounds small or medium-size squid
2 tablespoons olive oil
3 red bell peppers
6 anchovies, halved
1 tablespoon capers
DRESSING:
2 tablespoons whole-grain mustard
1/4 cup lemon juice
Salt and pepper, to taste
2 garlic cloves, finely chopped
1/2 cup olive oil

1. Rinse squid, then holding the head just below the eyes, gently pull away from the body pouch. Discard the viscera that come away with it; carefully remove the ink sac and discard. Pull out the quill-shaped pen, which is loosely attached to the inside of the pouch, and discard.

2. Cut the head from the tentacles just below the eyes; discard head. Cut out the small round cartilage at base of tentacles. The tentacles will be in one piece. In the center is a long beak-like mouth; remove by squeezing with the fingers.

3. Skin the body pouch by slipping the fingers under the skin and peeling it off. Remove the edible fins on either side of the pouch. Rinse thoroughly under cold running water; dry well.

Slice the squid. In a saucepan, heat oil, add squid and cook gently 10 to 15 minutes; cool. Broil bell peppers until the skin is charred. Cool, then peel off skin. Cut peppers in half, remove stems and seeds and slice thinly. In a salad bowl, mix together squid, bell peppers, anchovies and capers. Whisk dressing ingredients together and stir into salad. Cover and refrigerate 1 to 2 hours before serving.

Makes 6 to 8 servings.

Squid with Vegetable Bundles

1-1/2 pounds small or medium-size squid
Salt
BATTER:
1-1/2 cups self-rising flour
1 tablespoon sesame seeds, toasted
Vegetable oil for deep-frying
TO SERVE:
2 carrots
4 ounces daikon
3 zucchini
Chives
Japanese soy sauce

1. Clean squid (see opposite page), then slice in thin rings. Wash well, sprinkle with salt and leave to drain in a colander 15 minutes. Dry well with paper towels.

2. Sift flour and a pinch of salt into a bowl. Stir in sesame seeds, then gradually add 1 cup cold water, beating constantly to form a smooth batter. Add squid and stir until coated.

3. Cut vegetables in thin matchsticks. Place a few sticks of each vegetable together and tie in bundles with a chive.

Heat oil to 350F (175C) or until a 1-inch bread cube turns golden-brown in 65 seconds. Add squid in batches and deep-fry 1 to 2 minutes, until golden-brown and crisp; drain on paper towels. Serve immediately, with the vegetable bundles and tiny dishes of soy sauce for dipping. Serve as a starter or a light meal.

Makes 4 servings.

Squid & Tomato Casserole

2 pounds small or medium-size squid
3 tablespoons olive oil
2 onions, chopped
1/4 cup brandy
2 garlic cloves, crushed
1 pound tomatoes, chopped
1 cup red wine
Bouquet garni
1 teaspoon paprika
Dash of Tabasco sauce
Salt and pepper, to taste
Pinch of sugar
1 to 2 tablespoons chopped parsley

1. Clean squid (see page 102), then slice thinly. In a skillet, heat oil, add squid and fry gently 10 minutes. Remove with a slotted spoon and set aside.

2. Add onions to the skillet and fry 5 minutes, until softened. Add brandy and boil rapidly to evaporate the alcohol. Add remaining ingredients, bring to a boil, then simmer, uncovered, 15 to 20 minutes, stirring occasionally, until thickened. Discard bouquet garni.

3. Press the sauce through a sieve, then return to the pan. Add the squid. Bring to a boil, then cover and simmer gently 45 minutes, until the squid is tender.

Sprinkle with parsley and serve with saffron rice.

Makes 4 servings.

Note: Substitute 1 (14-oz.) can chopped tomatoes for the fresh tomatoes.

Braised Squid with Olives

1-1/2 pounds small or medium-size squid
3 tablespoons olive oil
1 onion, sliced
2 garlic cloves, chopped
1-1/2 pounds tomatoes, peeled and chopped
1 bay leaf
2 fennel stalks
3/4 cup dry white wine
Salt and pepper, to taste
2/3 cup pimento-stuffed olives
TO GARNISH:
Fennel sprigs

1. Clean squid (see page 102), then slice in rings. Preheat oven to 325F (160C). In an flameproof casserole dish, heat oil, add onion and garlic and fry gently 10 minutes, until lightly colored. Add squid and fry gently 5 minutes.

2. Add tomatoes, bay leaf, fennel, wine, salt and pepper. Bring to a boil,

then cover and cook in the oven 1-1/4 hours, until squid is tender.

3. Remove bay leaf and fennel and stir in olives. Reheat gently; check seasoning. Garnish with fennel sprig and serve with steamed rice.

Makes 4 servings.

Stuffed Squid

2 large squid
Salt and black pepper, to taste
1/4 cup olive oil
1/2 onion, finely chopped
8 ounces spinach, shredded
1 red bell pepper, chopped
1/2 cup long-grain rice
1/3 cup pine nuts
3 tablespoons raisins
2 tablespoons chopped parsley
2 pounds tomatoes, peeled, seeded and chopped
1/2 cup dry white wine
1 teaspoon sugar
TO GARNISH:
Lemon twists and parsley sprigs

1. Preheat oven to 350F (175C). Grease a shallow ovenproof dish.

Clean squid (see page 102). Rub squid pouches liberally with salt and rinse well under cold running water. Chop tentacles into small pieces.

2. In a medium-size saucepan, heat half the oil, add the onion and fry gently about 10 minutes, until softened; add tentacles and fry 5 minutes. Add spinach, cover and cook gently 3 to 4 minutes, until wilted.

Stir in bell pepper, rice, pine nuts, raisins, parsley, salt and black pepper. Stir well, then remove from heat.

3. Two-thirds fill squid pouches with the mixture; sew up the ends. Put into prepared dish.

In a saucepan, combine tomatoes, wine, remaining oil, sugar, salt and black pepper. Bring to a boil, cover and simmer 10 minutes. Pour the tomato sauce over the squid, cover dish tightly and cook in the oven 1 hour, until tender.

Remove thread from squid. Cut each one in half and arrange on warmed plates. Garnish with lemon twists and parsley to serve.

Makes 4 servings.

Greek Octopus Salad

1-1/2 pounds octopus
1 cup hearty red wine
2 tablespoons red wine vinegar
2 teaspoons honey
2 oregano sprigs or 1 teaspoon dried leaf oregano
1 garlic clove, crushed
Salt and pepper, to taste
3/4 cup ripe olives
1/4 cup olive oil
2 tablespoons chopped parsley

1. Hold octopus firmly by head. Using a sharp knife, cut through flesh below eyes, severing head from tentacles. Turn body pouch inside out and discard viscera. Wash well under cold running water. Pick up tentacles; with index finger underneath the center, push the beak up and cut it away.

2. To tenderize tentacles, beat with a mallet until they feel soft and have lost their springiness. Remove any scales left in the suckers.

Plunge octopus into a pan of boiling salted water 5 minutes; drain well and let stand until cool enough to handle.

Using a sharp knife or scissors, cut octopus in 1-inch pieces. Put into a saucepan with no extra liquid and heat gently until it produces its own liquid. Increase the heat a little until the liquid has evaporated, then add wine, vinegar, honey, oregano, garlic, salt and pepper. Bring to a boil, cover and simmer 1 hour, or until tender.

3. Leave octopus in pan until cool, then with a slotted spoon, transfer to a serving dish; add olives. Mix 1/2 cup cooking liquid with olive oil. Pour over octopus and sprinkle with parsley. Serve with lettuce leaves.

Makes 4 to 6 servings.

Peppered Octopus

1 pound octopus, cleaned and boiled (see page 107)
6 tablespoons olive oil
1 bay leaf
1 small onion, quartered
1 teaspoon black peppercorns
Few parsley stems
2 garlic cloves, finely chopped
2 teaspoons paprika
1/4 teaspoon ground chile
1/2 red bell pepper, finely chopped
Salt, to taste
TO SERVE:
Lime wedges

1. Using a sharp knife or scissors, cut octopus in 1-inch pieces. In a large pan, put 4 cups cold water, 2 tablespoons oil, bay leaf, onion, peppercorns and parsley stems. Bring to a boil, add octopus, cover and simmer 1 to 1-1/4 hours, until tender. Drain, reserving 1/2 cup cooking liquid.
2. In a skillet, heat remaining oil, add garlic and fry gently 2 minutes. Add octopus, paprika, ground chile, bell pepper and salt. Stir well, cover and cook 2 minutes.
3. Add reserved liquid and cook, uncovered, until slightly reduced. Serve warm with toasted French bread or cold as a salad on a bed of shredded lettuce, accompanied by lime wedges.

Makes 4 servings.

Octopus in Wine

2 pounds octopus, cleaned and boiled (see page 107)
2 tablespoons lemon juice
3 tablespoons olive oil
2 teaspoons coriander seeds, crushed
1 onion, thinly sliced
1 leek, thinly sliced
2 garlic cloves, crushed
2 tomatoes, peeled and chopped
1 thyme sprig and 1 marjoram sprig
2 cups dry red wine
2 tablespoons tomato paste
Salt and pepper, to taste

1. Preheat oven to 325F (160C). Using a sharp knife or scissors, cut octopus in 1-inch pieces. Put into a bowl with lemon juice and leave 1 hour.
2. In an flameproof casserole dish, heat oil, add coriander seeds, onion, leek and garlic and cook over low heat 10 minutes.
3. Add octopus and fry, stirring, 2 minutes. Add tomatoes, herbs, wine, tomato paste, salt and pepper and bring to a boil. Cover the casserole tightly and cook in the oven 1 to 1-1/4 hours, until the octopus is tender. Remove herb sprigs. Serve with rice or steamed potatoes and a crisp green salad.

Makes 4 to 6 servings.

Octopus in Spiced Coconut Cream

1-1/2 pounds octopus, cleaned and boiled (see page 107)
1 coconut
2 tablespoons sunflower oil
3 tablespoons lemon juice
1 lemongrass stalk
2 gingerroot slices
Salt and pepper, to taste
2 teaspoons ground cumin
2 teaspoons paprika
2 green onions, shredded

1. Using a sharp knife or scissors, cut octopus in 1-inch pieces; set aside.

Pierce the two "eyes" in the coconut with a sharp skewer and drain off the liquid; set aside.

2. Crack open the coconut and remove flesh. Peel off the brown skin. Chop flesh and place in a blender or food processor with reserved coconut liquid and 1 cup cold water. Process until finely chopped, then strain through a sieve.

3. In a saucepan, heat oil, add octopus and fry quickly until it starts to turn pink. Add lemon juice, cover and cook gently 10 minutes, then add coconut milk, lemongrass, gingerroot, salt, pepper and spices. Bring to a boil, then cover and simmer gently 45 minutes, until octopus is tender; remove gingerroot and lemongrass.

Transfer to a warmed serving dish and sprinkle with green onions. Serve with steamed rice.

Makes 4 servings.

Cuttlefish Sofrita

2 pounds cuttlefish
2 tablespoons olive oil
1 onion, finely chopped
2 tablespoons chopped parsley
2 tablespoons chopped celery leaves
1 garlic clove, crushed
12 ounces spinach, shredded
1 pound tomatoes, peeled, seeded and chopped
Salt and pepper, to taste

1. Wash cuttlefish thoroughly, then place bone-side down on a board. Slit the mantle with a sharp knife, open carefully and discard the viscera and cuttlebone. Remove the ink sac.
2. Remove the skin from the flaps, then cut the mantle and flaps in 2-inch squares; score squares in a diagonal crisscross.
3. Cut off tentacles from below the eyes and remove beak. The edible parts of the cuttlefish are the two flaps, mantle and the tentacles. Chop the tentacles if using.

In a large pan, heat oil, add onion and fry 5 minutes, until softened. Add parsley, celery leaves, garlic and spinach. Cover and cook 2 to 3 minutes, until the spinach is wilted.

Add cuttlefish, tomatoes, salt and pepper and bring to a boil. Reduce heat, cover and simmer 20 to 30 minutes, until cuttlefish is tender. Serve with steamed rice.

Makes 4 servings.

Fisherman's Soup

2 pounds mussels, cleaned (see page 12)
2 cups dry white wine
2 tablespoons butter
1 leek, white part only, chopped
1 pound tomatoes, peeled, seeded and chopped
Strip of lemon peel
1 pound sea scallops
Salt and pepper, to taste
4 ounces peeled shrimp, thawed if frozen
1/4 cup whipping cream
2 tablespoons chopped fresh mixed herbs (e.g., fennel,
chives, tarragon, dill)

1. Put mussels into a large saucepan with wine and 1 cup water. Cover and cook over high heat, shaking pan, 3 to 4 minutes, until shells have opened; drain, reserving cooking liquid. Discard any that have not opened. Remove mussels from shells and set aside.

2. In a large saucepan, melt butter, add leek and cook gently about 5 minutes, until softened. Add tomatoes, lemon peel, half the scallops and 1/2 cup reserved cooking liquid. Bring to a boil, reduce heat, then simmer 10 minutes; remove lemon peel. Transfer mixture to a blender or food processor and purée until smooth.

3. Return purée to a clean pan and add remaining cooking liquid. Bring to a boil and season with salt and pepper. Detach corals, if present, from remaining scallops and cut the white part of each scallop into 4 pieces. Add scallops, corals, shrimp and mussels to the pan and simmer 5 minutes. Just before serving, stir in cream and herbs and warm through.

Makes 4 servings.

Variation: Replace mussels with clams.

Seafood Treasure Chest

6 ounces puff pastry, thawed if frozen
Beaten egg, to glaze
1/2 cup dry vermouth
3 egg yolks
3/4 cup butter, melted and cooled
1 tablespoon chopped cilantro
Salt and pepper, to taste
12 ounces shelled bay scallops
4 ounces peeled cooked small shrimp, thawed if frozen
TO GARNISH:
8 cooked shrimp in shells (optional)

1. Preheat oven to 425F (220C). On a lightly floured surface, roll out pastry and cut in 4 (5" x 3") rectangles. Put on a dampened baking sheet and slash across top diagonally several times; brush with beaten egg. Bake 12 to 15 minutes, until puffed, crisp and golden-brown. Keep warm.

2. In a small saucepan, boil vermouth until reduced by half; cool slightly, then put into a heatproof bowl with egg yolks. Set over a pan of simmering water and whisk together about 10 minutes, until mixture thickens. Slowly whisk in melted butter to form a sauce. Add cilantro, salt and pepper and keep warm over the water.

Steam scallops 3 to 4 minutes, until just firm. Add shrimp and steam 1 minute to heat through. Add to the sauce.

3. Split the pastry boxes in half horizontally. Put the bottoms on 4 warmed plates, spoon over the sauce and cover with the pastry lids. Garnish with whole shrimp and serve immediately, as a starter or light meal.

Makes 4 servings.

Seafood Terrine

4 ounces spinach leaves
1 (1-1/2-lb.) lobster, cooked
1 (1/4-oz.) package unflavored gelatin
1 (8-oz.) package cream cheese, softened
1/4 cup brandy
2 tablespoons lemon juice
2 cups whipping cream
Salt and pepper, to taste
8 ounces crabmeat (white and brown)
1 tablespoon chopped dill
YOGURT SAUCE:
1/2 cup plain yogurt
2 teaspoons chopped dill
2 teaspoons chopped fresh mint
TO GARNISH:
Dill sprigs and lemon twists

1. Blanch spinach in boiling water 1 minute; drain thoroughly and pat dry. Use spinach leaves to line a 9" x 5" loaf pan or mold, overlapping the edges. Remove lobster meat from shell (see page 32).

Break up shell and put into a saucepan with 3/4 cup water. Simmer 15 minutes; strain. Sprinkle gelatin over hot liquid; stir until dissolved.

2. Put lobster meat and half of the cream cheese, the brandy, the lemon juice and the gelatin mixture into a blender or food processor and blend until smooth; turn into a bowl. Whip cream until soft peaks form and fold half into the mixture. Season with salt and pepper. Turn into prepared mold and smooth the top; re-frigerate.

Blend crabmeat with remaining cheese, brandy, lemon juice and gelatin mixture. Turn into a bowl and fold in remaining whipped cream, with dill, salt and pepper.

3. Pour crab mixture carefully over lobster mixture and smooth. Fold spinach leaves over top to enclose and cover and refrigerate about 3 hours, until set.

To make sauce, mix together yogurt, dill, mint, salt and pepper. Turn out terrine and cut into thick slices. Garnish with dill and lemon. Serve with yogurt sauce.

Makes 6 to 8 servings.

Marinated Seafood Kabobs

12 sea scallops
12 small shrimp, peeled
12 large shrimp, peeled
2 garlic cloves
2 tablespoons chopped parsley
1 tablespoon chopped basil leaves
2 tablespoons lime juice
1/4 cup olive oil
Salt and pepper, to taste
1 cup bread crumbs, toasted
TO SERVE:
Lime wedges

1. Rinse scallops, removing any dark strands, and pat dry; detach corals. Cut white part of each scallop in 2 circles. Put into a bowl with small and large shrimp. Soak bamboo skewers in water.

2. Finely chop garlic and put into a pestle and mortar with herbs. Pound together to form a paste, add lime juice and pound again. Gradually work in oil to form a thick sauce; season with salt and pepper. Pour over seafood and mix well. Cover and re-frigerate at least 1 hour. Preheat broiler.

3. Thread scallops and shrimp alternately onto 4 skewers and sprinkle with bread crumbs. Cook under preheated broiler 6 to 8 minutes, until bread crumbs are golden and seafood is firm; turn several times during cooking. Serve hot, with lime wedges and rice pilaf.

Makes 4 servings.

Fritto Misto di Mare

8 large shrimp
16 small shrimp
8 ounces small squid, cleaned (see page 50)
Seasoned flour for coating
1/2 cup *each* self-rising flour and cornstarch
1/2 teaspoon baking powder
Salt and pepper, to taste
1 egg, beaten
1 cup iced water
1 head radicchio
1 small fennel bulb
1 tablespoon pine nuts
2 tablespoons French dressing
Vegetable oil for deep-frying
Lime slices to garnish

1. Peel shrimp, leaving tail sections intact. Cut down the back to remove dark vein (see pages 26 and 30). Cut squid pouch and tentacles in thin rings and fins in strips. Toss all seafood lightly in seasoned flour; shake off the excess.

Sift flour, cornstarch and baking powder into a bowl; add salt and pepper. Make a well in the center and add egg and a little iced water. Beat to incorporate dry ingredients; gradually add more water, beating well, until a smooth light batter is formed.
2. Separate radicchio leaves. Shred fennel and radicchio finely. Arrange on the side of 4 plates. Sprinkle with pine nuts and drizzle over a little French dressing.
3. Heat oil to 350F (175C) or until a 1-inch bread cube turns golden-brown in 65 seconds. Dip seafood into batter and deep-fry in batches 2 to 3 minutes, until crisp and golden. Drain well on paper towels and keep hot, while cooking the remaining seafood.

Arrange seafood on the plates and garnish with lime slices. Serve immediately, as a starter or light meal.

Makes 4 servings.

Seafood Platter

1 pound mussels in shells, cleaned (see page 12)
8 to 12 oysters
1 tablespoon pink peppercorns
8 to 12 crab claws
1 small cooked lobster, halved (see page 32)
1 pound cooked shrimp in shells (see page 26)
RED PEPPER SAUCE:
2 red bell peppers
2 tablespoons olive oil
Dash of Tabasco sauce
Salt and pepper, to taste
DILL SAUCE:
1 tablespoon chopped dill
2 tablespoons finely chopped cucumber
1 tablespoon white wine vinegar
3/4 cup dairy sour cream

1. Put mussels into a large pan with just enough water to cover. Cover pan and cook over high heat about 3 minutes, until shells have opened, shaking the pan occasionally. Drain and discard any that have not opened. Cool, then remove the empty half shells.

2. Pry open oysters (see page 14) and sprinkle a few pink peppercorns into each shell. Chill all shellfish and have ready plenty of ice.

To make Red Pepper Sauce, cook peppers under a broiler until charred all over. Wrap in foil and leave to cool, then remove skin and seeds and roughly chop flesh. Put into a blender or food processor with oil, Tabasco sauce, salt and pepper, and blend until smooth. Turn into a small serving bowl.

3. To make Dill Sauce, in a small serving bowl, mix together dill, cucumber, vinegar, cream, salt and pepper.

Arrange the seafood on a large platter with plenty of ice. Serve with the dill and red pepper sauces, and lemon and lime wedges. Accompany with thinly sliced dark rye bread.

Makes 4 to 6 servings.

Spanish Seafood Stew

1 pound mussels in shells, cleaned
12 clams in shells, cleaned
1/2 cup dry white wine
Salt and pepper, to taste
1 pound small squid, cleaned (see page 50)
4 cooked langostinos
3 tablespoons olive oil
1 onion, chopped
2 garlic cloves, crushed
1 tablespoon lemon juice
8 ounces tomatoes, peeled and quartered
1/4 cup sherry
8 ounces peeled shrimp, thawed if frozen
1 tablespoon chopped parsley

1. Put mussels, clams, wine, salt and pepper into a large pan. Cover and cook over high heat about 4 minutes, until shells have opened; discard any that do not open. Strain, then return liquid to pan and boil until reduced by half. Remove the mussels and clams from their shells.

2. Slice squid in rings. Remove shells and dark veins from langostinos (see page 30).

In a saucepan, heat oil, add onion and garlic and fry gently until softened. Add squid and fry gently 10 minutes. Add lemon juice, tomatoes, reduced cooking liquid, sherry, salt and pepper and bring to a boil. Reduce heat, cover and simmer 10 minutes, until squid is tender.

3. Add langostinos, mussels, clams and shrimp; stir and cook 5 minutes. Sprinkle with parsley to serve.

Makes 4 servings.

Seafood in Cider Sauce

2 cups dry cider
1 onion, chopped
1 carrot, chopped
Bouquet garni
Salt and pepper, to taste
3 pounds mussels in shells, cleaned (see page 12)
1-1/2 pounds large shrimp
12 live crayfish
2 egg yolks
1/2 cup whipping cream
6 tablespoons butter, in pieces
6 ounces button mushrooms
2 tablespoons lemon juice
TO GARNISH:
Chervil sprigs and croûtons

1. Combine cider, onion, carrot, bouquet garni, salt, pepper and 1 cup water in a large saucepan. Bring to a boil, then cover and simmer 10 minutes. Add mussels, cover and cook over high heat 4 to 5 minutes, until shells have opened. Remove with a slotted spoon and discard any unopened ones. Remove mussels from shells.

Add shrimp and crayfish to the pan and cook about 5 minutes, until shells are pink. Remove with a slotted spoon and cool in cold water. Peel crayfish and shrimp, leaving on tail shells. Devein shrimp.

2. Strain cooking juices into a pan and boil until reduced by three-quarters. Blend egg yolks and cream with a little of the cooking juices. Stir in pan and cook gently 5 minutes, or until thickened; stir constantly and do not boil. Remove from heat and whisk in butter a little at a time, until glossy.

3. Put mushrooms, lemon juice and 2 tablespoons water in a small saucepan and cook gently about 5 minutes, until softened.

Arrange seafood and mushrooms on a warmed serving plate and pour over the sauce. Garnish with chervil and croûtons to serve.

Makes 4 to 6 servings.